# WORLD FILM LOCATIONS LOS ANGELES

Edited by Gabriel Solomons, Jared Cowan and Fabrice Ziolkowski

T0277386

First Published in the UK in 2024 by Intellect Books, The Mill, Parnall Road, Fishponds, Bristol, BS16 3JG, UK

First Published in the USA in 2024 by Intellect Books, The University of Chicago Press, 1427 E. 60th Street, Chicago, IL 60637, USA

Copyright ©2024 Intellect Ltd

Cover photo: Summit Entertainment / The Movie Stills Database

Copy Editor: MPS Limited

Production editor: Sophia Munyengeterwa

A Catalogue record for this book is available from the British Library

**World Film Locations Series**
ISSN: 2045-9009
eISSN: 2045-9017

**World Film Locations Los Angeles Vol.2**
Paperback ISBN: 978-1-83595-029-6
ePDF ISBN: 978-1-83595-031-9
ePUB ISBN: 978-1-83595-030-2

Printed and bound by Short Run

# WORLD FILM LOCATIONS LOS ANGELES VOL.2

EDITORS
Gabriel Solomons
Jared Cowan
Fabrice Ziolkowski

SERIES EDITOR & DESIGN
Gabriel Solomons

CONTRIBUTORS
Jared Cowan
Robert Foulkes
Georgina Guthrie
David E. James
David B. Lyons
Neil Mitchell
Andrew Nock
Ada Pîrvu
Thomas M. Puhr
Sandy Reynolds-Wasco
Peter Schulman
Gabriel Solomons
David Wasco
Alberto Zambenedetti
Fabrice Ziolkowski

LOCATION PHOTOGRAPHY
Jared Cowan
(unless otherwise credited)

PUBLISHED BY
Intellect
The Mill, Parnall Road,
Fishponds, Bristol, BS16 3JG, UK
T: +44 (0) 117 9589910
F: +44 (0) 117 9589911
E: *info@intellectbooks.com*

Previous: Grauman's Chinese Theatre (Jared Cowan)
This page: South Seas Apartments (Jared Cowan)
Overleaf: Vista Theatre (Jared Cowan)

# CONTENTS

## DEDICATION AND ACKNOWLEDGEMENTS

GABRIEL SOLOMONS wishes to thank all of the wonderful contributors to this second volume who provided their fantastic depth and wealth of knowledge.

JARED COWAN wishes to thank Michelle and Brooklyn for their love and support as well as the film professionals who find endless cinematic inspiration throughout the City of Los Angeles.

FABRICE ZIOLKOWSKI wishes to thank Luli Barzman for her support through thick and thin and Steve Roberts for his acumen, acuity and astuteness.

# INTRODUCTION

## *World Film Locations* Los Angeles / Volume 2

**GABRIEL SOLOMONS:** When we launched the World Film Locations (WFL) series back in 2011, with volumes on Los Angeles, New York, Paris and Tokyo, the world was a different place. Although interest in film locations has grown steadily for years as people seek to walk in the footsteps of their cinematic idols by visiting sites from their favorite movies – the recent global lockdown seems to have only increased an appetite for cinetourism; prompting us to consider a second volume for one of the world's most evocative and enduring locations. The city of Los Angeles, with its meandering sun-baked sweep and beautifully fractured topography, continues to lure filmmakers into its clutches – affording an endless panoply of locations to prop up both character and story. Since 2011, thousands of new productions have made the most of what the city has to offer; using, reusing and discovering places that will surely become sites of pilgrimage in years to come – and while this volume includes just 50 of them, our modest selection is carefully curated to compliment volume 1 and further reveal both the well-known and more hidden parts of a Los Angeles in constant flux. We hope you enjoy the journey.

**JARED COWAN:** In 2005, I moved to LA from New Jersey, a transcontinental migration that I share with so many others, including the pioneers of the early twentieth century's burgeoning film industry. Funnily in LA I notice more license plates from Jersey than from any other state. Over the last ten years, I've written a lot of words, both in this book and elsewhere, on the subject of LA film locations. I sort of fell into writing on the subject journalistically after many days of driving sun-drenched streets and freeways to photograph the places that I had seen on screen or from worn VHS tapes or slightly smudged DVDs 3000 miles away. Hobby turned to profession and weekend joyrides suddenly turned serious, late-night deadlines. Though in the past I've preferred letting photographs articulate my passion for film locations, I've found that I'm often caught up in writing about the emotion, feeling and form vs. function implementation that locations conjure and convey. Upon setting foot at these places, they seem to belong only to me even, if but for a few fleeting moments. Sure, this could be said of filmed backdrops anywhere in the world, but the enduring character of locations is nowhere as intrinsic or palpable as in LA. The cinephile in me keeps this in mind when I start to think, *I'd have way less traffic to deal with back in New Jersey.*

**FABRICE ZIOLKOWSKI:** Los Angeles is tailor-made for love–hate relationships. I've loved it from afar for what it promised and hated it up close for what it didn't quite deliver at times – and those see-saw feelings are still there today. This book has been an opportunity to revisit and share those places, films, scenes, sounds and images. LA often feels like a place where you want to get lost, like in that old Chet Baker song. But you can also find out that it's impossible to hide there. So say Cassavetes, Altman, Varda, Wenders and many of the other filmmakers found in these pages. Some with drama, some with comedy, but all of them with a specific take on the place. For those who live in the heart of the beast, this might deliver a few keys to understanding the gap between how things are represented and the way they really are. For those who haven't been there yet, there are Sly Stone's immortal words: to get to it, you've got to go through it! ✢

# ROBERT ALTMAN'S LA

*The City of Fallen Angels*

Text by
FABRICE
ZIOLKOWSKI

**THE INTERIOR OF AN AIRLINER** approaching LAX. It's been a long flight and the first-time traveller to Los Angeles peers out the window, a little apprehensive but mostly mesmerized by the seemingly endless unfurling of the city below: millions of people, stories and interconnections. Is there hope of ever getting to the essence of the tangled web that lies down there? Luckily the newbie visitor who had the foresight of packing three films by Robert Altman is just a little more prepared to make some sense of the megalopolis magma that awaits.

Robert Altman's (1925–2006) filmography ranges far and wide in a variety of geographical directions (Paris, the American West, NYC, Kansas City, Nashville, etc.) and time periods (*Thieves Like Us*, 1974 *M\*A\*S\*H\**, *1970*). Within this teeming body of work stand three films that capture part of the ephemeral quicksilver nature of Los Angeles. Altman's LA is peopled with an anachronistic existential hero in *The Long Goodbye* (1973), with lost souls of various social statuses and origins in *Short Cuts* (1994) and with an array of venal movie industry characters in *The Player* (1992). With each film, Altman builds

on the daunting project of capturing the city's zeitgeist alongside other filmmakers like Polanski, Friedkin and Mann.

## THE LONG GOODBYE

In his 1973 *The Long Goodbye*, Altman tackles the monument that is Raymond Chandler – the foremost LA pulse-taker back in the late 1940s and 1950s. And while the term 'mean streets' is usually associated with Martin Scorsese and New York, the phrase originates in Chandler as he describes LA's atmosphere of corruption and violence, presenting Philip Marlowe as 'a man who is not himself mean'. Altman's stab at Chandler's 1953 *The Long Goodbye* revives Philip Marlowe from his earlier milieu and drops him into post-hippie LA. It's only twenty years later, but it feels like an eternity. Yet what Chandler had decried in his work, mainly the corruption of the city and the hall of mirrors it creates where nothing is quite what it seems, is still operative.

Police corruption is not on the menu in Leigh Brackett's updated screenplay that keeps Marlowe in a time loop, stuck in an early 1950s attitude and dropped in a post-Flower Power and Charles Manson era. Chandler's Marlowe used to care, but for Altman's iteration, things have changed. 'It's OK with me', he keeps repeating in an apparent live-and-let-live attitude. But that's just a façade that comes crashing down in the film's finale. The mean streets have changed somewhat: Marlowe's apartment stands next door to ditzy hippy women, Century City is the hangout of the mobster (whose origins have been transformed from Italian to Jewish) and the Malibu Colony is a hotbed of sexual shenanigans mixed with overflowing booze, charlatan shrinks and other shady characters. A 'modern' setting of Chandler with a 'modern' LA, in direct contrast with *Chinatown* – shot only a few months later.

## SHORT CUTS

Adapted from Raymond Carver short tales of ordinary lost souls, of disengagement and angst, this is a perfect fit for the LA environment Altman explores in what many consider to be his masterpiece. But disconnection is only a surface phenomenon in LA. A reminder that what qualifies as a 'surface street' in Los Angeles is any thoroughfare that is not a freeway. In other words, flying down the freeways affords you only a superficial view of what's going on. The connections only appear when you get down to the surface of things, when you take an off-ramp.

Altman argues that everyone actually is connected in one way or another and if they're not, they desperately want to be. Strange bedfellows and redemption abound. All of Carver is here though displaced from the Pacific Northwest to Southern California. But while Carver's characters are totally disconnected, Altman tries to link them all somehow in a kind of web, making them fit into the city's mosaic. Carver sets his people down in anonymous places, no addresses, no city names. Altman pins them down to specific LA locations as in the case of Lily Tomlin and Tom Waits who live in Downey. In all three of these films, Altman travels far and wide through LA, but actual filming locations slip through our fingers, always hard to pin down. We're constantly on the move. Like those helicopters that zoom through the sky above the fray in the film's opening title sequence. Taking a cue

**There is a nagging reminder that in LA more than anywhere else, you are what your car is. And if that happens to be a clown-car, well that's just your bad luck.**

from the credit sequence of *M\*A\*S\*H\**, Altman revisits a ballet of helicopters crisscrossing the nighttime sky, this time spraying malathion to eradicate the elusive medfly down below. A sequence that both takes us back to the COVID pandemic and other disasters on the cusp of which the city is always finding itself. There's also a clear implication that LA is a war zone where love is a battlefield: cowardice, jealousy, lust, envy, sisterly or motherly love.

Finally, there is a nagging reminder that in LA more than anywhere else, you are what your car is. And if that happens to be a clown-car, well that's just your bad luck.

## THE PLAYER

It's easy to be hard on the movie industry in LA. Michelangelo Antonioni once quipped that Hollywood is like being nowhere and talking to nobody about nothing.

And so Altman takes a big bite at the hand that feeds him with *The Player*. This could be the quintessential mean-spirited film about the movie industry set in its epicentre – though there are other serious contenders for that dubious honour including *Sunset Boulevard* (1950) or *The Big Knife* (1976). The film industry can be a serpent that bites its own tail and here Altman is gloriously spitting in the soup. A sort of antidote to *La La Land* (2016) and closer to the acerbic humour and cynical viewpoint of *Barton Fink* (1991).

It all begins with a virtuoso long take of 7:43 minutes over the credits. It's a sweeping panorama of the studio from interior to exterior and back again – a tip of the hat to *Touch of Evil* (1958) shot across town in Venice. A tour de force which turns the backlot and offices of the film studio into a stifling and maddening labyrinth from which there seems to be no escape: projects are pitched, people are fired, murder threats are received. It concludes with the cynical realization that even when it comes to betrayal and murder, Hollywood finds a way to recycle its worst impulses into yet another movie.

Altman's is a cubist vision of the city, trying to present varying angles that show an ever-fragmented whole. You can always try stepping back to see the pattern of the photomosaic or the Rorschach test. And as our traveller lands and enters the flow of LA traffic, they realize that they're just another facet of the picture. ❧

# LOS ANGELES LOCATIONS

## SCENES
## 1-8

# INTOLERANCE (1916)

*The Vista Theater, 4473 Sunset Drive, Los Feliz*

**CONSIDERING HIMSELF** the victim of narrow-mindedness following the attacks on his violently racist *Birth of a Nation* (1915), D. W. Griffith embarked on the mammoth *Intolerance* spanning various historical ages with a title that spoke his rancour loud and clear. The Babylon sequence featured the largest and most expensive set ever built at the time with 3000 extras and eight massive elephants. The culmination of the set's use is no doubt the breathtaking tracking shot from a 30-metre tower that descends on Belshazzar's feast. Lit and photographed by master cinematographer Billy Bitzer, the set stood for years after the film's completion in 1916 at the corner of Sunset and Hollywood boulevards. Over time, the abandoned set began to fall apart until it was finally destroyed in 1922. In 1927, a movie theatre was built in the very same location. The Vista Theater – which has its own rich history and is today owned by one Quentin Tarantino – now stands in the same hallowed spot. But ghosts die hard in Hollywood. Decades after the demolition of Griffith's Babylon set, it was partly recreated at the Sunset & Highland Center, a shopping complex some three miles away. Bemused visitors had a hard time figuring out where these extravagant elephant statues had come from – why they were there at all – albeit only two of the eight original pachyderms. A recent makeover of the shopping centre saw all traces of the *Intolerance* re-creation taken away, wiping out the last remnant of Babylon from Los Angeles. D. W. Griffith has left the building for good. **❧ Fabrice Ziolkowski**

*Directed by D. W. Griffith*
*Scene description: The feast of Belshazzar*
*Timecode for scene: 1:42:19 – 1:44:37*

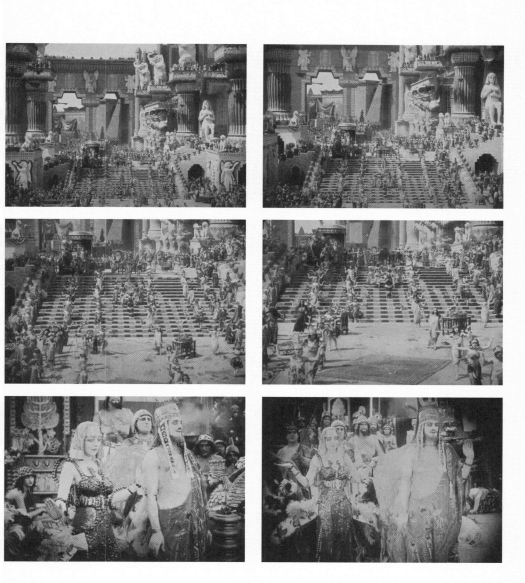

# TOUCH OF EVIL (1958)

LOCATION *Windward Avenue and Ocean Front Walk, Venice*

**FILM PROFESSORS** often teach of the art of the long take or, as it's known colloquially on a film set, the oner. When used organically, it's like a cinematic sleight of hand that not even the most seasoned film-goer is aware of until sometime after the shot has fully unspooled. In 1941, writer/director Orson Welles expanded the language of film with his magnum opus *Citizen Kane* by employing the camera in dynamic ways never before seen. Seventeen years later, it was Welles again who shattered the boundaries of camera choreography in his bleak, drug-fuelled film noir, *Touch of Evil*. In its much-studied opening long take, a homemade explosive device fills most of the frame as an unidentified man in a suit turns the timer to three minutes – about the length of the real-time shot. The bomb is hastily placed in the trunk of a 1956 Chrysler New Yorker convertible. As the camera cranes up and the Chrysler makes its way through the trash-strewn streets of the fictional border town of Los Robles, we're introduced to our newlywed protagonists, Mexican prosecutor Mike Vargas (Charlton Heston) and his no-nonsense bride Susan (Janet Leigh). The Chrysler is almost always in view before exploding on the US side of the border, punctuating the film with its first cut. The once-expansive Venetian-style colonnades of Venice Beach that were featured in *Touch of Evil* are – unlike Welles's opening shot – largely fractured today, with only a black-and-white mural keeping alive the full splendour of the location's on-screen visual character. ↬ *Jared Cowan*

*Directed by Orson Welles*
Scene description: A time bomb travels through a US-Mexico border town before detonating
Timecode for scene: 0:00:11 – 0:03:30

# THE SAVAGE EYE (1959)

*Angelus Temple, 1100 Glendale Boulevard, Echo Park*

**SHOT OVER A PERIOD** of four years and released in 1959, *The Savage Eye* is a dramatized documentary journey through Los Angeles that feels remarkably and oddly contemporary – between cinema verité and avant-garde film-making. Cinematographers Haskell Wexler, Jack Couffer and Helen Levitt capture the seedy side of the city in superb black-and-white footage as they follow divorcee Judith X (Barbara Baxley) through a personal odyssey in which she is haunted by a male voice-over. It's like a road movie through 1959 LA: a yoga class, a session of plastic surgery (a nose job to be more precise), a wrestling match, a visit to a strip club and its dressing rooms, and a gay masquerade ball. Judith's neurotic flight through the hostile urban environment prefigures John Cassavetes's *A Woman Under the Influence* and Antonioni's *Red Desert*. Street photographer Helen Levitt's work bears comparison with Robert Frank's downtown LA shots for the Rolling Stone's *Exile on Main Street* (1972) album cover. In the film's penultimate sequence, Judith is witness to a faith-healing session at the Angelus Temple built in 1927 by Aimee Semple McPherson, a Pentecostal evangelist who eventually fell from grace. Hers was the first mega-church built in America and could hold thousands. Today, faith-healing is no longer on the menu, but the Temple still holds services with over 8000 people attending weekly. As *The Savage Eye* ends, Judith turns her back on the obviously bogus faith-healing and leaves the city, hopefully moving towards a brighter future. •◆*Fabrice Ziolkowski*

*Directed by Ben Maddow, Sidney Meyers, Josef Strick*
*Scene description: Faith healers ministering to believers*
*Timecode for scene: 0:45:56 – 0:52:39*

# THE DAY OF THE LOCUST (1975)

*Grauman's Chinese Theater, 6925 Hollywood Boulevard, Hollywood*

**UNDOUBTEDLY ONE OF** the darkest films ever made about the movie industry from Nathaniel West's novel of the same name, the story focuses on various Tinsel Town outcasts at the tail end of the Great Depression. After exploring the seedy side of New York in *Midnight Cowboy* (1969), Schlesinger goes to town on Los Angeles. The cast of grotesque characters who are trying to make it in the business include young Yale graduate Tod Hackett (William Atherton), Faye Greener (Karen Black) and Homer Simpson (Donald Sutherland) all in striking but depressing performances. Schlesinger's adaptation swirls around various LA locations, most of which were barely still present in the 1975 film and now mostly vanished. The exception is the location for the film's apocalyptic ending that stretches over thirteen minutes and is set at the fictitious premiere of Cecil B. De Mille's *The Buccaneer* (1938) at Grauman's Chinese Theater. Homer, an asocial and perturbed accountant, finally snaps, murders a child and is torn apart by a mob in front of the theatre famous for its cement handprints. It's a gruesome pièce de resistance that mixes Dante's 'Inferno' with Goya's more horrific work with a dash of Munch's *The Scream*, and along with *They Shoot Horses Don't They* (Sydney Pollack, 1969), is one of the gloomiest films ever made about those lost souls who come to Hollywood and find only broken dreams. Built in 1927, Grauman's is an iconic location that has appeared in dozens of films and remains a major tourist attraction to this day.
➻ *Fabrice Ziolkowski*

*Directed by John Schlesinger*
*Scene description: The apocalyptic movie premiere*
*Timecode for scene: 2:06:08 – 2:19:54*

# ASSAULT ON PRECINCT 13 (1976)

LOCATION *685 N. Venice Boulevard, Venice*

**BY THE EARLY 1970S,** the Venice Division of the Los Angeles Police Department (LAPD) ceased operating out of an Art Deco, concrete fortress on Venice Boulevard that had been an active precinct since 1929. In 1977, it became the home of the Social and Public Art Resource Center, or SPARC, Los Angeles' preeminent cultural and social justice non-profit organization responsible for many of the city's murals. According to their website, SPARC is proud to have 'liberated' the building. But shortly before the visibly declining station could be rid of the ghosts of its former self, its decrepit and shuttered status provided the ideal setting for John Carpenter's urban western *Assault on Precinct 13*. California highway patrol lieutenant Ethan Bishop (Austin Stoker) is temporarily reassigned to supervise the final operating hours of the decommissioned Precinct 9 within the LAPD's Thirteenth Division. What should be a simple babysitting job turns into a nightmarish siege as a violent street gang seeks retribution for the death of one of their leaders. Carpenter sets up the location masterfully when Bishop arrives at the once-glorious and impenetrable police station. Taking in his surroundings as the setting sun casts an ominous orange glow, it's clear that the desolate streets of the fictional gang-ridden Anderson neighbourhood will provide no lifeline for what is about to transpire. With no electricity or working phone, the station might as well be the rickety wooden jail in *Rio Bravo* (Hawks 1959).
**↝Jared Cowan**

*Directed by John Carpenter*
*Scene description: A California Highway Patrol lieutenant surveys his temporary assignment*
*Timecode for scene: 0:16:38 – 0:17:51*

# THE BAD NEWS BEARS (1976)

*Mason Field, 10500 Mason Ave, Chatsworth*

**FEW LOCATIONS** play such an integral part in American movies as playing fields, since the drama of victory and defeat – with all the emotional baggage this entails – often unfolds on the hallowed ground of one sporting arena or another. For the Bad News Bears, a team of no-hope little league baseball players coached by a washed-up former minor leaguer and part-time pool cleaner Morris Buttermaker (Walter Matthau), their field of dreams happens to be Chatworth's Mason Field. It's here that the ragtag group of outsiders will be transformed into an actual title contender by the film's end, but not before both the team and Buttermaker discover that camaraderie brought about by trusting in one another will be a far greater victory in the long run than the mere lifting of a trophy. In the film's opening scene, the early-morning California sun settles on the carefully tended baseball field as Buttermaker arrives in his rickety 1964 Cadillac convertible, clearly the worse for wear as he hoiks a beer from his backseat cooler. Buttermaker, a cigar-chomping curmudgeon, has reluctantly agreed to coach the team for a fee, paid for by one of the wealthy and influential parents, Bob Whitewood (Ben Piazza), looking to get his unskilled kid some playing time. We're promptly introduced to the Bears and soon enough get a glimpse at their bumbling efforts when they take to the field for the first time. While it'll rely on the help of a talented but rebellious pair of teens (Tatum O'Neal as Amanda, and Jackie Earle Haley as Kelly) to propel the team's chances, the Bears' journey begins and ends on Mason Field, just one of a million modest baseball fields dotted around the country that provide a stage for a certain kind of American dream to play itself out. ➻ *Gabriel Solomons*

*Directed by Michael Ritchie*
*Scene description: Baseball season begins for the Bears*
*Timecode for scene: 0:00:15 – 0:11:15*

# HEAVEN CAN WAIT (1978)

*Los Angeles Memorial Coliseum, 3911 S. Figueroa Street, Exposition Par*

**ALL THAT HANDSOME**, charismatic Los Angeles Rams quarterback Joe Pendleton (Warren Beatty) wants to do is take his team to the Super Bowl. Easier said than done when Joe is killed in a car accident and, due to an after-life clerical error, placed into the body of another man named Leo Farnsworth, who also gets killed – er, murdered. When Joe learns that Tom Jarrett, the quarterback who replaced him, is suddenly injured and near death during the Super Bowl, Joe is granted a home inside Tom's body in order to complete and win the big game. The catch is, this final decision requires that Joe's memory be wiped clean, that he will henceforth only know himself to be Tom Jarrett. The film's final scene, one of several shots at the Rams' famed LA Memorial Coliseum, packs a surprisingly emotional wallop. Julie Christie's character, Betty Logan, had fallen for Leo – as played by Beatty – before his death, so when she runs into Tom Jarrett – also Beatty – alone inside a stadium tunnel after the big win, she has no idea who he is until Betty hears Tom say something touching that reminds her of Leo. The tunnel lights go out. A spiritual connection washes over her. They step outside, and the eyes of these two people who've never met – but we've seen together the entire movie! – profoundly connect. As they walk off together across a now empty field, falling in love again for the first time, the stadium lights gradually extinguish until the silhouette of the Coliseum's iconic peristyle is all that remains on-screen. **➤Robert Foulkes**

*irected by Warren Beatty and Buck Henry*
*ene description: A football stadium where a team wins and love endures*
*mecode for scene: 1:34:34 – 1:40:08*

# 1941 (1979)

Santa Monica Pier, end of Colorado Avenue, Santa Monica

**LOS ANGELES** has been destroyed in sundry ways throughout film history: earthquakes, tidal waves, volcanos, alien invasions. Steven Spielberg has his own rollicking good time in making Angelenos freak out over an attack by the Japanese Imperial Navy in his raucous *1941*. Though many locations in the city's geography are given a hard time, the Santa Monica Pier – the end of Route 66 – stands as the most iconic and damaged target. Never mind that most of the scene is shown at night and is largely recreated through miniatures and special effects, this is probably one of the best uses of the pier which has appeared in films for over a hundred years, the first feature being Mack Sennett's *Tillie's Punctured Romance* (1914) concluding with a chase and a gunfight. Most of the characters in the film are in a state of overexcitation about the attack and possible invasion. Three of them find themselves on the Ferris wheel attached to the pier which is in turn seen as a perfect target by the Japanese submarine commander (Toshiro Mifune) who blasts away at the fun ride. Watching the Ferris wheel roll down the pier and heading for the inevitable drop into the ocean, the submarine crew rejoices. The wheel finally drops over the edge of the pier in a visually and aurally similar manner as the truck that runs amok in Spielberg's feature debut *Duel* (1972). It's like a wounded dinosaur going over a deadly cliff and letting out a last agonizing shriek. Banzai! •*Fabrice Ziolkowski*

*irected by Steven Spielberg*
*scene description: Killing of the Ferris wheel at Santa Monica Pier*
*timecode for scene: 2:06:44 – 2:20:23*

# FRINGE BENEFITS

Text by
DAVID E.
JAMES

*The Spaces and Places of the LA Avant-Garde Cinema*

**OF THE CONDITIONS** that have affected non-commodity or avant-garde film-making in Los Angeles, two are especially important: the capitalist film industry itself and the variety and magnificence of the California landscape: the mountains and the desert, on the one hand and the unusual architectural features of the city itself, on the other. The changing interaction among these is best illuminated by an historically periodized survey.

In the 1910s and the 1920s, while the industry was in flux and the difference between studio and experimental film-making still porous, two important films made independently by studio workers exemplify these options: *The Soul of the Cypress* (Dudley Murphy 1920) and *The Life and Death of 9413: A Hollywood Extra* (Robert Florey, Slavko Vorkapich and Gregg Toland 1928).

Arguably, the first avant-garde film ever made, *Cypress* is the only surviving one of three 'Visual Symphonies'; films that Murphy made, heavily influenced by California Pictorialist photography and featuring a beautiful woman in a wild natural landscape. It featured Chase

Harringdine as a wood nymph dancing among the wind-swept trees of the Point Lobos natural reserve overlooking the ocean. *Hollywood Extra*, on the other hand, detailed the tragic fate of a would-be actor as he struggled through the streets and studios of Hollywood. All the film-makers involved in these went on to notable careers in the industry, though Murphy made an initial detour to Paris where he collaborated with Fernand Léger in making the Dada classic, *Ballet Mécanique* (1924).

The coming of sound in the 1930s ended the production and distribution of such semi-professional landscape films and, with the depression, independent film-making became completely non-commercial and politically agitational. The LA branch of the Workers Film and Photo League documented both the rural and urban environments of political activism: in Kern Country, with the striking cotton workers, San Pedro, with the striking dockers and many other working-class locations that had previously been neglected.

During the war, Maya Deren created the psychodramatic trance film, beginning the renewal of film-making that matured in the classic US avant-garde of the 1950s and 1960s. Employing a bungalow in Hollywood and also the beach, her *Meshes of the Afternoon* (1943) used the environment as a metaphor for interior trauma. Though she soon left for New York, her innovations were influential in LA, especially on Curtis Harrington who projected his own sexual anxieties on the city itself (*Fragment of Seeking*, 1946), on the desert (*On Edge*, 1949) and on the beaches (*Picnic*, 1948 and *Night Tide*, 1960).

The richness of LA's visual environment and especially some of its bizarre subcultures continued to be a resource for independent filmmakers, from the ferocious satire of *The Savage Eye* (Ben Maddow, Sidney Meyers and

Barbara McCullough opened a Black female perspective on the city in *Water Ritual # 1: An Urban Rite of Purification* (1980) in which a naked woman investigates the ruins of a house destroyed to accommodate a new freeway, and Nina Menkes similarly explored female trauma by visualizing it in menacing environments; her *The Bloody Child* (1996), for example, set its investigation of the murder of a woman in the Mojave desert and the towns that dot it. And Fred Halstead's *L.A. Plays Itself* (1972) depicted homosexual encounters in both the idyllic valleys of the Santa Monic Mountains and in the sleazy streets of Hollywood itself.

Effectively proscribed from identity politics, white heterosexual male filmmakers often turned to ambitious geographical projects, and around the turn of the century, Pat O'Neill, James Benning and Thom Anderson each produced magisterial trilogies of feature length works mobilizing the spatialities of LA and Southern California.

Each part of Benning's California Trilogy separately explores the state's natural world, its constructed world and the agricultural world where these interpenetrate. All are identically composed of 35, 2½-minute shots of landscape scenes made with a stationary camera. The first, *El Valley Centro* (1999), explores the fields and the towns of what used to be America's breadbasket, while *Los* (2000) is composed of vignettes in LA and *Sogobi* (2002) – the word for 'earth' in the Shoshone language – of beauty of the desert and mountains.

O'Neill had been working for many years with natural vistas similar to Benning's but his were typically transformed by industry-quality image manipulations, especially timelapse photography and multiple superimpositions. His *Water and Power* (1998), for example, superimposed the Owens Valley, where LA's water comes from, upon the city which was enabled to grow by appropriating it.

Thom Anderson's three-part *Los Angeles Plays Itself* (2003) is a montage of clips from more than a hundred feature films in which the city has appeared, first as a nonspecific backdrop to the narrative or second as the representation of some other place. Only in the last does he turn to films both shot and set in LA, where the city is itself the subject and where it actually 'plays itself'. ✤

Joseph Strick 1959) to the more measured and historically minded *L.A.X.* (Fabrice Ziolkowski 1980), both of which revealed distinctively eccentric urbanscapes.

After the 1960s minority filmmakers made avant-garde films that documented their own places, entirely avoiding the Hollywood that had rendered them invisible. Asian American filmmakers revealed Chinatown, Little Tokyo and other places in the city that had not been seen in films before. Bob Nakamura, for example, made *Manzanar* (1971), set in the Owens Valley desert where Japanese Americans had been interned during the war and *Hito Hata: Raise the Banner* (1980) that explored Asian American communities across California, but especially in LA. Chicano filmmakers similarly revealed new perspectives on East LA where the community had previously lacked representation; *Requiem 29* (David Garcia 1971) documented a police riot in an east-side park during the Chicano Mortarium against the war. But the most audacious and dramatic use of working-class spaces was made by African Americans. The hitherto unrepresented Black communities of South Central in Haile Gerima's *Bush Mama* (1976) and Charles Burnett's *Killer of Sheep* (1977).

Sexual minorities also saw themselves in their specific localities.

**fter the 1960s inority filmmakers ade avant-garde lms that documented eir own places, itirely avoiding e Hollywood that ad rendered them visible.**

# LOS ANGELES LOCATIONS

## SCENES 9-16

# L.A.X. (1980)

*East 5th Street towards Harbor Freeway, Downtown*

**MUCH OF WHAT THIS** and the previous volume on Los Angeles look to explore, is the way in which a city is portrayed at different times, in different locations and by different filmmakers. *L.A.X.* could be seen as one of the definitive 'city symphony' films on the subject, inasmuch as what we experience throughout is a layered investigation of the historical and social erasure that often accompanies a place's transformation over time. LA's desire to continuously reinvent itself takes on a particular significance when we remember that the city often exists most luminously onscreen – LA being the home of Hollywood and the 'Dream Factory'. But as with dreams, the reality lurks somewhere beneath, and Ziolkowski's film reminds us of the landscapes that have disappeared, the people that have been displaced and the cultures that have been supplanted while the bulldozers and cameras relentlessly roll on. Long tracking shots of familiar vistas from above and at street level are accompanied by varied narration adding personal and historical context – hinting more at what is no longer there than at what is visible. We turn from Stanford Avenue onto 5th Street in one of the film's longest scenes. Shot from inside a moving car and accompanied by Robert Johnson's devastatingly bleak 'Love in Vain'; shops, pedestrians, parking lots and restaurants fill the frame as we pass by Skid Row – known for its homeless population since at least the 1930s and one of the film's only locations to have changed very little in the subsequent near half-century – a telling reminder that some of the city's problems can't simply be airbrushed from our screens. ➻ *Gabriel Solomons*

*Directed by Fabrice Ziolkowski*
*Scene description: A long drive up 5th Street*
*Timecode for scene: 0:37:01 – 0:44:40*

# MUR MURS (1981)

*The Great Wall of Los Angeles – Tujunga Wash – Coldwater Canyon Avenue between Oxnard Street and Burbank Boulevard, Valley Glen*

**THE NUMEROUS ART PROJECTS** that blossomed on LA walls in the 1970s are at the heart of French filmmaker Agnes Varda's whimsical portrait/ journey through the city in her 1980 film, *Mur Murs*. In her inimitable style, Varda mixes a personal poetic voice-over with philosophical musings about walls, the traces left by artists, what it means to write and paint on walls, on cars and on one's body. A harbinger of her later work with street artist JR, this is no doubt her best LA film and a high point of a career crowned by an honorary Oscar in 2017. The film's most exciting focus is the artwork inspired by the muralist movement born in Mexico and led by José Clemente Orozco, David Alfaro Sisqueiro and Diego Rivera in the 1930s. Muralism was kept alive by an exceptional burst of creativity from the Chicano Power art movement. The major highlight of the film is Varda's exploration of the Great Wall of Los Angeles mural, credited as one of the longest murals in the world. The work shows the history of California from dinosaurs to the 1970s. It was completed over a period of five years by a multitude of artists, led by the Chicana muralist Judith Baca. Incidentally, Varda's film includes the so-called Pig Paradise mural of the Farmer John slaughterhouse in Vernon – a site that also appears in Brian De Palma's *Carrie* (1976). Considering the stench that used to emanate from this location (it was demolished in early 2024), visitors did well to stay with the Great Wall. **•►Fabrice Ziolkowski**

*Directed by Agnes Varda*
**Scene description: The Great Wall of Los Angeles**
*Timecode for scene: 0:23:33 – 0:27:32*

# THE DECLINE OF WESTERN CIVILIZATION (198.

*Club 88 (now defunct), 11784 W. Pico Boulevard, Sawtelle*

**LA'S VIBRANT** punk music scene is alive and well in Penelope Spheeris's documentary shot in late 1979 and early 1980. The scene was a lively affair featuring groups like X, Black Flag, the Circle Jerks, the Germs, Catholic Discipline and the emerging Red Hot Chili Peppers. Spheeris has conjugated the various facets of this revolutionary music and cultural scene through live performances shot in several clubs around Los Angeles and on a soundstage and some personal interviews. The film captures the movement as an outgrowth of the Sunset Strip micro rock ecosystem of the late 1960s and early 1970s. A not so gentle atmosphere, dangerous and violent at times, peopled with outcasts and angry young folk – several of whom have died since the film was made like Darby Crash who overdosed before the film's premiere. While you can still listen to the music today with your earbuds, sadly no actual physical vestiges of the scene's hot spots are to be found. Only phantom limbs remain of such iconic places as Al's Bar, the China Club and the Alligator Club. Still, one of the film's most brilliant sequences is the appearance of X at Club 88. The high-octane energy of the group is felt through the few numbers they perform here. The location of Club 88 is reportedly occupied today by a toy factory. However, one door down stands a new hip bar called Neat on the site of the much-missed Liquid Kitty. Time to indulge in a few shots of Old Overholt while listening to the Germs on your smartphone. No pogo dancing allowed.
➠ *Fabrice Ziolkowski*

*Directed by Penelope Spheeris*
*Scene description: X performs at Club 88*
*Timecode for scene: 0:58:02 – 1:07:07*

# THE STATE OF THINGS (1982)

LOCATION *Sunset, Hollywood and La Brea Boulevards*

**WHEN FICTIONAL** film director Friedrich Munro (a play on the name Murnau) finds himself in a pickle in the middle of a shoot in Portugal, he flies to Los Angeles to confront his producer and demand more money to finish the film. Shot in splendid black-and-white by Henri Alekan (the man who gave us Cocteau's *Beauty and the Beast*, 1947) when Wenders was on hiatus from directing *Hammett* for Francis Ford Coppola, the film's last half-hour stands as an ode to all those luckless souls who try to make sense out of LA's often disorienting grid and who perish when the streets of the city become a deadly existential maze. Friedrich finally tracks down Gordon to a mobile home in the parking lot of Tiny Naylor's at Sunset and La Brea (the restaurant was torn down in 1984). The next and last twenty minutes of the film unfold in this rolling studio set as the producer explains that he's hiding out because Mafia loan sharks want to kill him due to the film being in black-and-white. 'What happened to the color?' the idiots demanded to know. Sunset Boulevard in all its melancholy glory passes by in the background of the mobile home's picture windows as Gordon launches into an improvised musical lament about Hollywood and its illusions. The ride ends tragically for both Gordon and Friedrich as they return to the Tiny Naylor parking lot. Beware: catching this location is as elusive an exercise as grabbing sand. But just cruise the boulevards at night for a while and you'll get the picture. ➼*Fabrice Ziolkowski*

*Directed by Wim Wenders*
*Scene description: Friedrich meets Gordon*
*Timecode for scene: 01:48:55 – 01:52:00*

# FAST TIMES AT RIDGEMONT HIGH (1982

LOCATION

*Van Nuys High School at 6535 Cedros Avenue, Van Nuys*

**WHILE ADRIAN LYNE'S** fatalistic teen drama *Foxes* (1980) was an originator of films about pre-adult self-discovery in the San Fernando Valley, a film two years its junior set the bar for what would prove to be a moneymaking juggernaut for which 1980s American cinema is famous. Based on the non-fiction book by Cameron Crowe, who also wrote the screenplay, *Fast Times at Ridgemont High* would prove to be as funny as the poster suggested – Sean Penn's lovable stoner Spicoli sitting at a school desk surrounded a surfboard and two cheerleader types in short shorts – but didn't shy away from the true-to-life hardships and themes featured in Lyne's film. As the title suggests, the pressures of sex, popularity, success and conformity are all present under the roof of Ridgemont High, a fictional high school implied to be in the San Fernando Valley. Unlike *Fast Times'* mall interior, the Sherman Oaks Galleria, which was completely redesigned as a mix-use office, retail and dining complex about eight years after the 1994 Northridge Earthquake, Ridgemont High is very much still intact at Van Nuys High School. As the opening twang of Tom Petty's 'American Girl' rings loud, toilet paper is strewn about the trees, bushes and the high school's façade in a display of teenage contempt of educational institutionalism. Like the specimens about to be studied in Mr Vargas's biology class, the first day of school presents a microscopic view of the cliques, fashion trends and classroom authoritarianism that make up Ridgemont High. ➙ *Jared Cowan*

*Directed by Amy Heckerling*
Scene description: *The first day of school at Ridgemont High*
Timecode for scene: *0:06:28 – 0:14:39*

# TRON (1982)

*'Flynn's Arcade', Hull Building, 9543 Culver Boulevard, Culver City*

**IN TRON,** software engineer and computer hacker Kevin Flynn (Jeff Bridges) lives a life that for millions of game players would be the ultimate dream; owning his own arcade and living directly above it. One of the few real-world locations seen in a movie where the majority of the action takes place in the digital world, Flynn's Arcade is a vibrant extension of its owner. A neon-lit space of escapism, youthful vitality and fun, it's the perfect environment for the maverick talents of the smart, mischievous and charismatic Kevin. Flynn's Arcade stands in direct contrast to the cold, clinical and uber-corporate ENCOM headquarters, from where employees and romantic partners, Dr Lora Baines (Cindy Morgan) and Alan Bradley (Bruce Boxleitner), travel to visit Kevin. It is in Kevin's open-plan, Bohemian living space above the main arcade, that the trio concoct a scheme to combat the Machiavellian plan to pass Kevin's work off as his own devised by the ENCOM Senior Executive Vice President Ed Dillinger (David Warner). A vital sequence in *Tron*'s narrative trajectory, the visit to Flynn's Arcade also instils in the viewers' mind a tangible sense of the arcade's space and wider place within LA's physical environment. It is, however, illusory as there has never been an arcade situated at 9543 Culver Boulevard. Built in 1925 by Dr Foster Hull, the building named after the doctor was Culver City's first hospital, before becoming Freeman Furniture and The Bank of Orange County among other businesses and eateries and, as of 2018, is the home of the self-described 'rustic-chic' Akasha Restaurant. Despite its numerous real-world incarnations, for a generation of movie-lovers, the Hull Building at 9543 Culver Boulevard will always be Flynn's Arcade. **↦ Neil Mitchell**

*Directed by Steven Lisberger*
**Scene description: Lora and Alan visit Kevin at the arcade**
*Timecode for scene: 0:16:53 – 0:22:18*

# VALLEY GIRL (1983)

LOCATION | *Del Amo Fashion Center, 3525 W. Carson Street, Torrance*

**TO THE MAX.** *For sure. Gag me. Barf out. Grotty. Gnarly. Awesome. Bitchin. Dork.* Just some of the 'Valspeak' terms that Valley Girl Julie Richman (Deborah Foreman) and her three besties – um, not yet a term in 1982! – punctuate their dialogue within this opening scene that takes place – where else – in the food court of a shopping mall. Not the famed Sherman Oaks Galleria, as the film's opening and closing establishing helicopter shots lead the viewer to believe, but at the Del Amo Fashion Center 27 miles south down the 405 freeway. A location selected, as lore tells it, due to budgetary considerations, but also perhaps due to the Galleria having already been prominently featured in that other iconic, teenage-angst-in-the-Valley classic, *Fast Times at Ridgemont High*. While the unexpected Frank and Moon Zappa hit, also titled 'Valley Girl', pre-dates Martha Coolidge's film, this scene helped to further cement 'Valspeak' into our collective noggins right out of the starting gate. When Julie surprises her friends at the scene's conclusion by making fun of a woefully uninteresting Valley boy across the food court, she wistfully declares how she 'definitely needs something new'. That something arrives two scenes later on a Pacific Palisades beach in the hunky, shirtless form of one Nicolas Cage, blowing into her world – and future cinema – like the force of nature that he is. For sure. → **Robert Foulkes**

*Directed by Martha Coolidge*
*Scene description: Girls, food, boys and 'Valspeak'*
*Timecode for scene: 0:02:51 – 0:04:28*

# REPO MAN (1984)

*Under the 1st Street Bridge, Downtown*

**IF EVER A FILM** screamed 'punk comedy', this is it. Young Otto (Emilio Estevez) gets hired by a shady repo man (Harry Dean Stanton) and drives all over Los Angeles getting into trouble while looking for a purpose in life and a meaning to the universe. The boy has a lot on his plate. Filmed by Wim Wenders cinematographer Robby Müller, Otto's journey is a textbook case of downtown locations shot at a time when the art and punk scene were in their heyday and hipsters hadn't invaded the place yet. In a strange prefiguration of *The Matrix* (1999) and *The X-Files* (1998; complete with an Anna Wintour lookalike badass), the film kicks off with a stolen car barrelling down the highway with highly radioactive aliens in its trunk and a state trooper being vaporized. There are bleak streets, rundown cars, shifty characters, uptight bosses, dangerous gang members and generic products everywhere. A delightful menu which is topped by Miller (Tracey Walter) who philosophizes to young Otto under the 1st Street bridge, near the railroad yards and the LA river. It's all about those cosmic coincidences one comes up against throughout one's life and why they're there. A lattice of coincidence Miller calls it. Time machines and aliens, man. And he concludes that he doesn't want to learn how to drive, because 'the more you drive the less intelligent you are'. While most of the downtown locations of the film have been gentrified to smithereens, the LA river and its train tracks still stand as a perfect spot to explore existential questions.
→ *Fabrice Ziolkowski*

*Directed by Alex Cox*
*Scene description: A lattice of coincidence*
*Timecode for Scene: 0:33:03 – 0:35:43*

# THE HAPPIEST PLACE ON EARTH

Text by
ALBERTO
ZAMBENEDETTI

*Disneyland and the Cinematic Experience*

**DISNEYLAND IS NOT A FILM LOCATION,** at least not in the traditional sense. While the theme park's pristine reimagining of a downtown street in the American Midwest (Main Street, U.S.A.) would provide the perfect set for a Victorian romance, since the park's opening in 1955 this quaint space only appeared in Disney's own TV specials and in a brief scene in *Saving Mr. Banks* (John Lee Hancock 2013) – the same film also featuring a rare shot of the fanciful pastiche of European castles (most notably the Neuschwanstein Castle in Bavaria, Germany) that welcomes visitors to Fantasyland. In fact, many of Disneyland's famous rides, from Adventureland's Jungle Cruise to Tomorrowland's Space Mountain, from Fantasyland's Matterhorn Bobsleds to Mark Twain's River Boat in Frontierland, are not tied to, nor do they originate from, the world of Disney films. It is certainly true that some attractions, especially the dark rides of Fantasyland, were designed as a sequence of vignettes culled from the animated

features (Pinocchio's Daring Journey, Snow White's Scary Adventure), while others explicitly replicate a sensory scenario from the films' diegeses (Dumbo the Flying Elephant, Peter Pan's Flight). By the same token, some rides were retrofitted to accommodate characters and episodes from pictures that entered the Disney catalogue after they were built (Finding Nemo Submarine Adventure), or were even based on the attractions themselves (the Pirates of the Caribbean saga). In this respect, the park is always evolving, as Walt Disney wanted: for instance, the iconic Splash Mountain was initially based on the controversial *Song of the South* (Foster and Jackson 1946) and later rededicated to the more palatable *The Princess and the Frog* (Musker and Clemens 2009). More recently, entire sections of Disneyland were redeveloped to expand the universe of franchises such as Star Wars, a fruitful partnership that began with the Star Tours motion simulator in 1987.

Yet, there is no denying that the 30-feet-wide street linking Main Street's town square to the round plaza on which the theme park's spoke-and-wheel layout is centred *feels* like a movie set. The inaccessibility of most upper floors of the reassuringly scaled-down buildings reinforces this impression, as do the horse-drawn trolleys and period-inspired automobiles puttering by. Well before the red-brick sidewalks give way to the actual film-based attractions, park visitors are treated to a three-dimensional cinematic experience created by employing movie studio technology, not traditional building techniques. The forced perspective that channels the eye down Main Street and toward Sleeping Beauty's castle, as well as the music and popcorn smell filling the air, invite patrons to tune in, both

emotionally and sensorially, to the charms and thrills of the themed lands that lie ahead. Of course, Disney himself conceived of a visit to Disneyland as a narrative experience akin to a movie, with Main Street as 'Scene One'. And while the park continues to be updated according to the 'structural principle of the technological aestheticization of fluid motion', as Vanessa R. Schwartz has put it, it does so to protect and perpetuate this illusion: as it is well known, in order to create the most immersive experience possible, characters cannot cross into lands where they do not belong; all workers are de facto cast members of a day-long performance; the windy side streets lead back to the park's centre hub; and tall walls, trees and hedges block the view of the outside world. Disneyland is a cloistered space, a cocoon designed to provide the best spectatorial experience to patrons willing to suspend their disbelief, much like a dark movie theatre.

But unlike most amusement parks of yore, on which the Anaheim marvel is certainly inspired, Disneyland is not a motley assembly of rides, but a carefully planned venue laid out according to the tenets of narrative placemaking, an urban design philosophy that connects architecture and space through storytelling. In this respect, the park

## Disney himself conceived of a visit to Disneyland as a narrative experience akin to a movie, with Main Street as 'Scene One'

resembles (and improves upon) the pavilion-based structure of Universal Exhibitions, with which it also shares the striking visual impact, nationalist bent and utopian technophilia. In fact, Disney's Imagineers (a portmanteau of Imagination and Engineers) created ground-breaking attractions for the 1964 New York World's Fair that were later relocated to the park(s), such as Great Moments with Mr Lincoln, a historical figure revered by the entrepreneur, or Walt Disney's Carousel of Progress, which is now operating in Magic Kingdom Park in Florida. Employing Disney's trademarked Audio-Animatronics (speaking robotic figures), these attractions fit perfectly into Walt's original concept for Disneyland's Tomorrowland – the ride that originated the eponymous 2015 Brad Bird young-adult action film. While not necessarily of his own design, together with the gasoline-powered cars of Autopia (scheduled to be electrified by 2026), the accented birds of the Enchanted Tiki Room and the multicultural children of It's a Small World (also a World's Fair dark ride), they speak of an idea of America (and the world) that attests to Disney's Cold War-era secular humanism and steadfast trust in technological progress.

As an experiential locale, Disneyland engenders its own configuration of time and space (chronotope), manipulating its temporality in quintessentially cinematic fashion; as the inscription on its entryway reads: 'Here you leave today and enter the world of yesterday, tomorrow, and fantasy'. The present, with its worries and anxieties, is precisely what Disneyland encourages visitors to leave outside its gates. And unlike a traditional location, which exists before and after a film is shot there, and generally serves purposes *other than* being a location, Disneyland's only raison d'être is being *both* the location and the cinematic experience itself. Borne out of a past that never was (Main Street), a future that never will be (Tomorrowland) and a plethora of experiences arising from the movie world (Adventureland, Fantasyland, Frontierland), Disneyland is cinema incarnate, a total experience for users of all ages, made possible by a synergic entente between film-making know-how and visionary urban planning. ❧

SUN VALLEY

PASADENA

18

RESEDA          LAKE
                BALBOA

VAN
NUYS

NORTH
HOLLYWOOD

UNIVERSAL
CITY

GLENDALE

ENCINO

STUDIO
CITY

22

GRIFFITH PARK/
LOS FELIZ

21

PACIFIC
PALISADES

BRENTWOOD

BEL-AIR

HOLLYWOOD

LAKE

MALIBU

BEVERLY
HILLS

24

WEST
HOLLYWOOD

20

23

CHINA
TOWN

19

WESTWOOD

MID
WILSHIRE

KOREA
TOWN

CENTRAL
CITY

SANTA
MONICA

WEST LOS ANGELES

17

VENICE

CULVER CITY

VIEW PARK

WESTCHESTER
LAX

INGLEWOOD

WATTS

N

GARDENA

LOCATIONS MAP

LONG
BEACH

# LOS ANGELES

*Map used for guidance and reference only*

SAN
PEDRO

# LOS ANGELES LOCATIONS

## SCENES
## 17-24

# NIGHT OF THE COMET (1984)

LOCATION *El Rey Theatre, 5515 Wilshire Boulevard, Miracle Mile*

**THIS POST-APOCALYPTIC** slice of 1980s camp about a comet that wipes out life on Earth save for a few lone survivors was released at a time when it seemed fashionable to locate films in decaying Los Angeles landscapes. The fear of nuclear disaster continued to cast a dark shadow over even the most optimistic Reagan-era promises of growth and prosperity, and from this fear emerged grim filmic portrayals of a world that had gone to hell in a handbasket, lacking a funny bone or any glimmer of irony. *Comet*, a rare comedic exception, has as its leads a pair of feisty sisters that sidestep the lazy stereotypes and well-trodden tropes from a slew of prior B-movies, where teenage girls were ineffectual sidekick props for the lead at best and disposable eye candy at worst. Reggie (Catherine Mary Stewart) is the rebellious teen, a street-smart character in the Ellen Ripley and Sarah Conner mould (only with bigger hair and a curfew). Samantha (Kelli Maroney) is a cheerleader and a gutsy tomboy – all hip-swagger and gum-chewing sass, packing an (albeit jam-prone) Mac-10 machine gun and whip-smart banter. When we first meet her, Reggie is working as an usherette and general dogsbody at The El Rey movie theatre, the iconic venue preparing a midnight comet show for ill-fated folks to better witness the event. Fed up with being harassed by rowdy punters, Reggie and projectionist boyfriend Larry (Michael Bowen) opt for a sleepover in the projection room, and it'll be the room's steel-lined walls which save their lives, the pair oblivious of the Comet's cataclysmic effects while heavy petting through the night. Built in 1936 and designed by Clifford Balch, The El Rey lies in the heart of the Miracle Mile, one of LA's preserved art deco districts. The 770 capacity venue ran for over 50 years as a first run movie house before being converted into a live music venue in 1994. **⇢ Gabriel Solomons**

*Directed by Thom Eberhardt*
**Scene description: Reggie holes up in The El Rey overnight**
Timecode for scene: 0:01:58 – 0:10:43

# THE KARATE KID (1984)

LOCATION *South Seas Apartments, 19223 Saticoy Street, Reseda*

**FIVE YEARS BEFORE** Tom Petty sang about how dull and drab Reseda could be, Daniel (Ralph Macchio) and Mrs LaRusso (Randee Heller) travelled from New Jersey to Southern California to start a better life. Upon arriving at their new home, palm trees sprout through the frame as the camera widens and booms down to a standard San Fernando Valley apartment building, the South Seas. Its tropical name, however, cannot mask the humdrum uniformity of courtyard buildings built in the late 1950s and early 1960s to accommodate the urban sprawl of people moving farther out of the immediate LA area. Optimistic Mrs LaRusso talks about how great the new place is; Daniel notices the lacklustre paint, the dead tree stumps and perhaps the most depressing of all, the pool, which was drained of water specifically for the film. It's the perfect metaphor for the audience's perceived vision of sunny Southern California vs. the standard reality for millions of people that live there – the juxtaposition of the California Dream playing off of a monotonous, 37-unit building on a busy street next to a liquor store. Though the apartments have been remodelled many times over, the exterior, the pool and the lava rock fountain still exist as of this writing. The LaRussos's apartment interior was the film's only set constructed on a soundstage, but Mr Miyagi's (Pat Morita) confined workshop was built into one of the complex's carports, providing a heightened sense of reality for the actors. ⟿***David B. Lyons***

*Directed by John G. Avildsen*
**Scene description: Daniel and Lucille LaRusso arrive at their new apartment in the Valley**
*Timecode for scene: 0:03:33 – 0:08:57*

# BREAKIN' 2: ELECTRIC BOOGALOO (1984)

*Casa Del Mexicano, 2900 Calle Pedro Infante, Boyle Heights*

**IN THE CENTRE** of historic Boyle Heights lies Casa Del Mexicano, a 100-year-old, hemispherical domed structure that towers over a dead-end street, with palm trees running right up the middle. For over a century it has been a cultural hub, erected as a Methodist church, later becoming a synagogue and finally a Mexican community centre, changing with the demographics of the neighbourhood around it. By the time it was selected as the youth centre, 'Miracles', for *Breakin' 2*, it had already been a place of refuge for Mexicans seeking help during the great depression, a centre for education and a base for donation drives that have helped thousands. While the bright, primary colours that decorated it in the hit breakdance film are no longer there, it is still a magnificent centrepiece towering over the lower to middle-class homes around it. The location proved to be an inspired choice on the filmmakers' part for a beacon of hope. After a couple decades of mismanagement, a fight for the building ensued that runs somewhat parallel to the film's plot of the evil, greedy developers trying to displace the centre's kids and teachers – led by Ozone ('Shabba-Doo' Quinones), Turbo (Michael Chambers) and Kelly (Lucinda Dickey) – that want to bring a centre for dance and culture to their home. Currently run by the East LA Community Corporation and in a bit of life imitating art, it's been occupied by a dance troupe that focuses on teaching various forms of authentic Mexican dance. **⇢David B. Lyons**

*Directed by Sam Firstenberg*
**Scene description: Street dancing to Miracles, the hub of community youth culture**
**Timecode for scene: 0:09:22 – 0:09:35**

# BARFLY (1987)

*Bryson Apartments, 2701 Wilshire Boulevard, MacArthur Park*

**BARBET SCHROEDER'S** *Barfly* is a romantic paean to writer Charles Bukowski and his fictional alter ego Henry Chinaski – played here by Mickey Rourke with Faye Dunaway as Wanda, another luckless drifter. For those fans of Hank looking for his old haunts to get a whiff of where the old writer/boozer swilled down the hooch, there is disappointment ahead. The dive bars that appear briefly or at length in the film like The Golden Horn have mostly disappeared, that kind of watering hole having a limited lifespan. But take heart, other seedy bars pop up in Los Angeles all the time. The Rodeo Room (1306 S. Vermont) is a good candidate as is any other bar that doesn't have its own website. On the brighter side, the apartment building that housed Henry and Wanda's love nest still stands in all its glory. Built in 1913, The Bryson has stellar noir credentials and is famous as a location for a host of other films including *Double Indemnity* (Billy Wilder 1944) and *The Grifters* (Stephen Frears 1990). Written about by Raymond Chandler and owned for several decades by *Double Indemnity* star Fred MacMurray, it overlooks Lafayette Park. In *Barfly*, Chinaski bounces around the two sides of LA, the lowlife (a steady role as a barfly) and the potential high life (an unsteady role as a published author). The Bryson represents a middle ground between those two polar opposites. **•◦ Fabrice Ziolkowski**

*Directed by Barbet Schroeder*
*Scene description: Wanda and Hank have it out*
*Timecode for scene: 0:47:17 – 0:51:10*

# LESS THAN ZERO (1987)

*Tunnel T-1, 1701 Kanan Dume Road, Malibu*

**DIRECTOR MAREK KANIEVSKA** had a prolific career in British television from the mid-1970s to the early 1980s, but it's a wonder that the director didn't have a bigger career in Hollywood following the making of his stylish, pastel and neon-laced adaptation of Bret Easton Ellis's 1985 novel *Less Than Zero*. Kanievska follows in the tradition of the German and Eastern European directors who, following WWII, made the transition to the Hollywood 'Dream Factory' and that most 'LA' of genre pictures, film noir. Like other British filmmakers who have explored LA (*Blade Runner*, Scott 1982; *L.A. Story*, Jackson 1991), Kanievska's lens should not be simplified as an European's view of the city, but rather one that is constantly discovering, slightly on edge and utterly authentic. Desperately trying to find their best friend Julian (Robert Downey Jr), who's strung out from an excessive and expensive drug habit, Clay (Andrew McCarthy) and Blair (Jami Gertz) approach two twin tunnels swallowed by the salt air darkness of a Malibu mountainside. At the south end of the western tunnel is a lit work zone where, ironically, no one is at work; a coyote crosses the path of Clay's red, 1960 Corvette. They're certain they've hit it, but somehow the coyote has escaped its demise. While the tunnel is arguably less visually impressive than some of the film's iconographic, modernist and faux neoclassical architecture, LA's tunnels go hand in hand with the development and expansion of the city's freeway system. **↝ Jared Cowan**

Image © Google

*Directed by Marek Kanievska*
*Scene description: Two teen lovers confront the realities of the moment*
*Timecode for scene: 1:02:39 – 1:04:38*

# SOME KIND OF WONDERFUL (1987)

LOCATION  *Hollywood Bowl, 2301 N. Highland Avenue, Hollywood*

**WITH THE PULSATING BEAT** of drums, the rhythmically set opening montage of *Some Kind of Wonderful* cuts from one image to another, from one character to another. Tomboy Watts (Mary Stuart Masterson) plays the drums while Keith (Eric Stoltz) plays chicken with a train … in a scene that you can't really beat from this 1980s teen movie. To the charged atmosphere of 1980s music, we are shown a suspenseful love triangle, with characters that are individuals dealing with coming-of-age angst that feels personal and not manufactured. This story does something to you. Music is such a big part of somebody's personal story, especially of that emotionally charged time of life when the stakes seem so high, and the music is what connects you to each character, every song matching beat for beat each sequence. When Keith finally takes Amanda (Lea Thompson) out on a date and enlists his best pal Watts to act as chauffeur, unaware of her affections, they end up at the Hollywood Bowl. Keith and Amanda sit on the stage and he gives her the diamond earrings while Watts is watching from the cheap seats. Since its opening in 1922, the Hollywood Bowl has been the foremost destination for live music in Los Angeles, hosting everyone from Judy Garland to The Beatles and Bob Dylan. Carved into the bowl-shaped area of the Hollywood Hills, making for excellent natural acoustics, America's most famous band shell had its original set of concentric arches (still featuring in the film) replaced with a larger one in 2003. It is an epic place, equally in significance and size. Howard Deutch shoots it wide then starts to close in on it, and in that tightened width of a deserted Hollywood Bowl you feel Watts's emotional anguish, as she watches her entire world (she has previously confessed that her drums and Keith are the only things she cares about) crash down before her eyes. ➜ *Ada Pîrvu*

*Directed by Howard Deutch*
*Scene description: Keith gives Amanda the diamond earrings*
*Timecode for scene: 1:17:21 – 1:22:00*

# THEY LIVE! (1988)

LOCATION *Edward R. Roybal Learning Center, 1200 Colton Street, Westlake*

**THEY LIVE!,** John Carpenter's paranoid LA set satire based on the 1963 short story 'Eight O'clock in the Morning' by Ray Nelson, in which bug-eyed aliens live among us unseen due to subversive mind control, acts like a wake-up call to apathetic America dulled into passive obedience through mass consumerism, and an all pervasive marketing assault. Thus, screens are everywhere in the film – from the TV sets that regurgitate inane branded fluff in a seemingly endless loop, to the advertising billboards plastered around the city. Into this anaesthetized landscape drifts a nomadic, unemployed alpha-male called Nada (played by alpha-male pro wrestler 'Rowdy' Roddy Piper) who stumbles upon the covert alien invasion with the help of truth revealing sunglasses (the iconic 'Hoffman' lenses). Nada is at first a reluctant hero, seeing himself as a good citizen who 'believes in America', but a chance meeting with fellow drifter Frank (Keith David) and the arrival of the pair into Justiceville, the city's makeshift haven for the downtrodden and destitute, will open his eyes in more ways than one. The shantytown, with its ramshackle scenes of despair, lies in the shadow of the sparkling high rises of downtown, ominously looming as if mocking the pair while Frank lays out his theory about the corrupt system that creates an economically divided society. It's in this key location that Nada's journey truly begins and where he will uncover the resistance group with which he'll later partner in an effort to unmask and overthrow the alien conspiracy. Little is now left of the original shooting location, as the plot on which Justiceville was created is now the soccer field of the Edward R. Roybal Learning Center, named after the first Latino LA City Councilman of the twentieth century, who vigorously fought for equal education in his district.
**Gabriel Solomons**

*Directed by John Carpenter*
*scene description: Nada and Frank enter Justiceville*
*timecode for scene: 0:08:44 – 0:11:42*

# MIRACLE MILE (1989)

*La Brea Tarpits and Museum, 5801 Wilshire Boulevard, Miracle Mile*

**ON 30 OCTOBER 1938**, Orson Welles's live radio broadcast of *The War of the Worlds* sparked panic as listeners were convinced of an impending alien invasion. Welles tapped into a primal fear of a world on the brink of war and utilized the trusted media of the day to lend authenticity to his illusion. *Miracle Mile* posits a similar scenario when mild-mannered Harry (Anthony Edwards) becomes privy to a possible nuclear invasion when he answers a payphone outside of an LA diner. Having met the potential love of his life Julie (Mare Winningham) hours earlier at the La Brea Tarpits, Harry subsequently fails to make their midnight rendezvous and so races to the diner in the hope of catching her. The panicked call which he receives after leaving a message on Julie's answerphone sparks a series of events that lead to citywide chaos and a growing concern on Harry's part that the whole thing may have been a hoax, and he the hapless rube who set cataclysmic events in motion. The La Brea Tarpits, with their primordial displays of mammoths descending into black ooze, provides the perfect spot to bookend a film about imminent extinction, and its location as part of the Miracle Mile neighbourhood lends the film its cryptic title. In a city so preoccupied with living in the moment; often whitewashing its past in an effort to perennially reinvent itself, the La Brea Tarpits are a reminder of where, not just Los Angeles came from, but from where everything emerged and to where it can just as easily return if we're not careful.
➝ *Gabriel Solomons*

*Directed by* Steve De Jarnatt
*scene description:* The Beginning and the End
*timecode for scene:* 0:04:51 – 0:05:46 and 1:20:56 – 1:23:30

# (DIS)TASTEFUL APPEARANCES

## *The Architecture of Seduction in* Twilight

**Text by PETER SCHULMAN**

**ROBERT BENTON'S ELEGIACAL** neo-noir showcases both his stellar cast of aging movie stars, Paul Newman, Gene Hackman, Susan Sarandon and James Garner as well as the modernist architecture they inhabit in order to highlight Benton's vision of a decaying, ruthless Hollywood wrapped up in facades of elegance and grace. During the opening credits we see the silhouette of Susan Sarandon's character, the faded film star Catherine Hayward, leisurely swimming in her gorgeously turquoise pool. It is at the centre of the Art Deco house she lives in with her husband, Jack Ames, once a movie star as well but now dying of cancer. As both Harry Ross, Paul Newman's character, an ex-gumshoe who lives with them, and her husband look on, Hayward encompasses the beguiling seduction that Hollywood glamour still exercises on a city engulfed in crime and corruption even as she orchestrates the murders of several characters who come close to exposing

the couple's involvement in the murder of her first husband twenty years before.

Benton focuses on three architectural gems with connections to the film industry: the 1930s era Dolores Del Rio house in Pacific Palisades, John Lautner's modernist George Jacobsen House near Mulholland Drive (which overlooks Universal Studios and the San Fernando Valley where many films were shot) and Frank Lloyd Wright's Arch Oboler House (Oboler was an old Hollywood radio playwright and screenwriter) in Malibu. All three are metaphors for Benton's notions of Hollywood power built on greed and immorality despite tasteful appearances. The interiors of the Del Rio house, for example, were designed by the fabled film star Dolores Del Rio's husband, Cedric Gibbons, who was a production designer. In *Twilight* (1998), Benton highlights the house's vast modern windows to underline the spectatorship the narcissistic couple indulge in (the house is also filled with portraits and pictures of a younger Hayward) while Ross is the outside who, similar to Joe Gillis in Billy Wilder's *Sunset Boulevard* (1950), lives over the garage. Yet throughout the film, he is the one who sees clearly and is able to pierce the ugliness behind the illusions. When he conducts his own investigation after being shot at during a suspicious errand Ames sends him on, he uncovers the years of cover-ups and mischief hidden below the beautiful homes he encounters. Jack Hope, a retired colleague and friend (played by Garner), who has been paid handsomely for years to keep the Ames involvement in the murder a secret, lives in the Jacobsen home with its panoramic views of LA's skyline. As in so many other LA-

based films, in which gangsters and criminals own sterling, modernist homes, Hope clings to the feeling of being 'above the smog' and when Ross comes to visit, he tries to urinate on him as a joke from his perch. Benton's long shots of Los Angeles at twilight then at night are reminiscent of David Lynch's portending shots of Mulholland Drive in his iconic 2001 film. Similar to Lynch's vision, Benton's perspective from the Jacobsen House represents the aspirations but also the sinister deeds some people are willing to commit in order to achieve them.

The third space Benton features is the Ames' ranch house, the Arch Oboler home designed by Frank Lloyd Wright overlooking Malibu. Just like the Lautner house Hope uses as symbol of his triumph over a city that seems so accessible and controllable through the house's transparent walls, the Oboler home is also glass endowed and dominates its views yet is isolated and remote enough to hide the murdered corpse that Ross and his assistant excavate. When Hayward surreptitiously comes by to make sure all is in order, it is at twilight of course, 'the magic hour' of movies but also an apt metaphor for the twilight of the actors portrayed in the film, if not an

**As in so many other LA-based films, in which gangsters and criminals own sterling, modernist homes, Hope clings to the feeling of being 'above the smog'...**

allusion to Wagner's 'twilight of the gods'. The film is hardly Wagnerian or bombastic, however, but known for its slow, elegant pace. *Twilight*'s melancholia is punctuated by Elmer Bernstein's blue and wistful score. Even the characters' names point to lost glory and dissipating illusions. Catherine Hayward evokes the great actor Susan Hayward; Jack Hope points to notions of hope not completion (or the comedic actor Bob Hope); Ross is sent to deliver a payoff to a certain Gloria Lamar (a name that can be read as a combination of Gloria Swanson and Hedy Lamarr); the strong perfume Hayward wears (and serves as one of the proofs of her involvement in the murders) is an old-fashioned scent called Bal à Versailles (it was created in 1962) that alludes to the Palace of Versailles where French aristocrats and monarchs romped before the French Revolution.

'Doesn't it bother you that the Jacks and Catherines do as they please because there's always guys like you and me who clean up after them?' Hope asks Ross when Ross figures out his role in the murder Hayward is trying to stifle. 'It's them and there's us', Hope continues, 'I couldn't give up this place, not then, not now.' Of course he wouldn't give it up no matter how much blood he has to spill, just as, more discretely, Catherine wouldn't sacrifice the protected confines of the Del Rio House. If *The Maltese Falcon* ends with Humphrey Bogart famously cradling the sought-after falcon which he identifies as 'the stuff dreams are made of', the dreams of the *Twilight* characters are more vague. Hope fights for comfort and control; Hayward hangs on to a cocoon of marital love, long ago fame and a safety insured by money and power. Only Ross, the recovered alcoholic, is devoid of such desires and is able to see through all the glass from the Julius Shulman-like shots of the three featured houses. 'You know I can see your reflection in the glass', Ross remarks to Hope who is about to shoot him. 'Funny the things you don't think about when you're buying a house,' Ross concludes. Fortunately, Benton has thought of them in this mise-en-abîme of four brilliant legends portraying four fading ones. ❖

# LOS ANGELES LOCATIONS

## SCENES 25-32

# PRETTY WOMAN (1990)

LOCATION *Cicada, 617 S. Olive Street, Downtown*

**WHEN HIGH-POWERED** corporate raider Edward Lewis (Richard Gere) invites the man whose company he's eyeing for a hostile takeover out for a nice dinner, his restaurant of choice is the uber-elegant 'Voltaire'. In actuality, it's a fine-dining establishment known as Cicada (Rex il Ristorante at the time of filming), located inside the Oviatt Building, a downtown LA Art Deco masterpiece completed in 1928 and still well worth the visit. Ed's attorney, Phil (Jason Alexander), suggests that Edward keep the dinner social, to bring a date. Little does Phil know that accompanying Edward will be Vivian (Julia Roberts), a gorgeous yet extremely unsophisticated hooker whom Edward's paying to spend the week with him. Vivian's never set foot in a restaurant like Voltaire, made abundantly clear during their five-course meal, including a comedic moment that helped cement Roberts as America's Sweetheart – the accidental flinging of her escargot into the hands of an unsuspecting waiter. Though, by the time the final course arrives, Vivian has learned something more important than how to manoeuvre her way through an elegant meal – witnessing firsthand what a cutthroat businessman Edward is. Perhaps surprisingly, Edward doesn't express embarrassment or frustration with Vivian's lack of sophistication during what otherwise could have turned into an over the top, slapstick scene in less assured hands than director Garry Marshall's. His interest lies more in how this key scene steers these mismatched romantic characters into deeper revelations, summed up in the following scene by Edward to Vivian: 'We're both very similar. We both screw people for money.' **➥ Robert Foulkes**

Directed by *Garry Marshall*

*Scene description: Edward and Vivian try to have an elegant dinner*

*Timecode for scene: 0:51:44 – 0:56:30*

Images © 1990 Touchstone Pictures

71

# TERMINATOR 2: JUDGEMENT DAY (1991)

*Southwest corner of Hayvenhurst Avenue & Plummer Street, North Hills*

**BY THE EARLY 1990S**, Los Angeles was the bank robbery capital of the world. The city's sprawling freeway system was, in the eyes of a master criminal, made for a daring getaway. As a result, LA car chases have been explored in dozens of films and continue to be central set pieces of LA action movies. But when you take the chase off the freeway and into a suburban community, the result is ultimately more spectacular – and more personal. Early scenes of *Terminator 2* feature orange-tinged streets, single-storey ranch homes and a mention of 'the Galleria'. Though it's never formally spoken, these elements point to the San Fernando Valley, where a young John Connor (Edward Furlong), the future hero of the Terminator universe, is growing up with an adoptive family. Two Terminators are sent back through time to locate John: the familiar and hulking T-800 – once again played by Arnold Schwarzenegger – and the highly advanced, liquid metal T-1000 (Robert Patrick). After a one-on-one mall brawl between both Terminators reveals that the T-1000 is out to do harm and the T-800 is likely trying to protect John, our young hero manages to escape on his motorcycle, racing through the streets of the Valley. The T-1000 hijacks a semi-truck and follows him to a dried-up drainage wash. The truck ploughs through a street-level concrete guard wall, over the embankment and crashes into the wash below, where a high-octane chase ensues between David and Goliath. ➻ *Jared Cowan*

*Directed by James Cameron*
*Scene description: An unforgettable Valley intersection*
*Timecode for scene: 0:30:07 – 0:30:59*

# GRAND CANYON (1991)

LOCATION *'Lem's Automotive Service', 4155 W. Washington Boulevard, Arlington Heights*

**TO LIVE AND SURVIVE** in Los Angeles. *Grand Canyon* is about breaking up ever-widening social and personal barriers in an edgy LA that struggles to bridge the divide between classes and races. Mack (Kevin Kline), a white immigration lawyer, takes a different route home one evening when his car breaks down in a crime-ridden neighbourhood of LA. He finds himself threatened by a Black gang. But a kind tow-truck driver, Simon (Danny Glover), another Black man, arrives and helps diffuse the tense situation. Soon after, as the two sit at a local gas station waiting for the car to be fixed, Simon brings up the Grand Canyon, which lends the film its title, while musing on the hardships of making a life and surviving another day in LA: 'The thing that got me was sitting on the edge of that big old thing. When you sit on that edge you realise what a joke we people are. Those rocks were laughing at me and my worries. It makes you feel small.' It's the moment that sets in motion a series of interwoven stories about characters from both sides of a racially segregated LA. Convinced that Simon saved his life that night, Mack returns to the gas station, determined to make something more of that fortunate encounter. A friendship maybe. By film's end, the two of them will drive together with their families to the Grand Canyon, little specks brought together by life and sympathy sitting on the edge of those old rocks. ➜ **Ada Pirvu**

*Directed by Lawrence Kasdan*
*Scene description: Talking about life in LA and sitting on the edge of the Grand Canyon*
*Timecode for scene: 0:21:22 – 0:25:06*

# WHITE MEN CAN'T JUMP (1992)

LOCATION *Lafayette Park, MacArthur Park*

**JUST TO THE WEST** of downtown Los Angeles, and merely two blocks away from MacArthur Park, sits Lafayette Park. A smaller park in an urban setting, the land was a partial tar pit donated to the city by the Shatto family who, at the time, owned Catalina Island. Trees were immediately planted in order to give it a less urban feel. Originally named Sunset Park, the name was changed around the onset of World War I to recognize Marquis de Lafayette, a Major General of the American Revolution. The park now features two courts, one of which was constructed and left by the film company of *White Men Can't Jump*, a very uncommon practice due to the ever-present fear of liability after production has wrapped. The ample tree coverage along with midrise commercial and residential buildings surrounding the park provide a stark contrast to the beachfront and South Central courts featured in the film. It helps to tell the story of two basketball hustlers who simply want better lives and aren't afraid to hustle to obtain them. The tournament is the legitimate version of their street games that so often devolve into threats of razor blades and guns. The best in the city come here to compete, and our heroes come away victorious. The courts are seen again in the final game of the film, where our heroes, Sidney Deane (Wesley Snipes) and Billy Hoyle (Woody Harrelson), come take on the nearly mythical hustlers that have come before them. You can still play on the courts today, which appear almost exactly as they did in the film.
**➫ David B. Lyons**

*Directed by Ron Shelton*
*Scene description: Sidney and Billy compete in a two-on-two basketball tournament*
*Timecode for scene: 0:58:47 – 1:10:31*

# BLOOD IN, BLOOD OUT (1993)

LOCATION *'El Pino' at N. Indiana Street & Folsom Street, East Los Angeles*

**BLOOD IN, BLOOD OUT** is the epic story of three family members raised in East Los Angeles who's diverging paths we follow over the course of twelve turbulent years. In the film's opening scenes Miklo (Damian Chapa) returns to LA after a bust up with his white father, reuniting with cousins Paco (Benjamin Bratt) and Cruz (Jesse Borego). When asked where he'd like to go first Miklo responds 'El Pino' – and it's at the site of this large bunya pine, overlooking the familiar streets of their youth that Miklo feels most at home. Soon after, the cops arrive, reminding us of the oppressive daily routine most young people in this part of LA are subject to. El Pino – which has become an international ambassador for the area thanks in large part to it featuring in *Blood In, Blood Out* – is a fitting metaphor for the three young men who are bound by common Chicano roots to East LA, yet branch off in different directions. Paco will become a cop, Cruz an artist and Miklo a gangster; each of them embodying a particular lived experience with all the complex dynamics forged through a life of struggle. It's Miklo's journey however, propelled by his need to be wholly accepted as Chicano, which tells us the most about the need for belonging – and the violent lengths some will go to achieve it. And such is the cultural significance of El Pino to both the area's residents and people the world over, that when a prank announcement of the tree's imminent removal was posted back in late 2020, petitions were signed and a flood of angry letters of complaint were sent to the city's mayor demanding it be saved. **⊷Gabriel Solomons**

*Directed by Taylor Hackford*
**Scene description: Miklo's return to the city and paying a visit to an old friend**
**Timecode of scene: 0:11:15 – 0:14:20**

Images © 1993 Hollywood Pictures

# BOWFINGER (1999)

LOCATION *1621 Vista Del Mar Avenue, Hollywood*

**THE INDIE NEW WAVE** of the 1990s coincided with plans for an urban renewal of Hollywood Boulevard, a tourist destination at which tourists generally spent very little time due to its reputation for drugs, homelessness and prostitution. Parts of *Pretty Woman* (Marshall 1990) could almost be considered documentary film-making. At the same time filmmakers of the 1990s were famously maxing out credit cards (*Clerks*, Smith 1994) or becoming lab rats (*El Mariachi*, Rodriguez 1992) to fund their movies, proposals for a rejuvenated Hollywood were in the works. Through location, *Bowfinger* perfectly encapsulates Hollywood redevelopment of the era and the maverick spirit of the decade's filmmakers. Bobby Bowfinger (Steve Martin) runs a failing, inconsequential production company, Bowfinger International Pictures, out of a 1922 Spanish bungalow-style home tucked into the armpit of a Hollywood backstreet. An establishing crane shot of the house shows it surrounded only by parking lots connecting to Hollywood Boulevard. Other than a cheap motel and a couple of other small homes adjacent to his, Bowfinger feels like the last holdout on a block about to be gentrified. A last ditch effort to make a movie, without the star actor knowing he's in it, eventually pays off with the bizarrely titled *Chubby Rain*. No longer surrounded by parking lots, it's almost as if Bowfinger still resides in the house today, surviving amidst the sprawl of modern midrise apartment buildings. He's still a holdout, but a holdout whose rejuvenated career has afforded him the ability to remodel his once-crumbling production office. ⟿ *Jared Cowan*

Directed by Frank Oz
Scene description: The home of Bowfinger International Pictures
Timecode for scene: 0:05:36 – 0:05:44

# TRAINING DAY (2001)

**FLANKED ON ONE SIDE** by Sunset Boulevard and on the other by Dodger stadium, the property situated at 1031 Everett Street has afforded a commanding view of downtown Los Angeles since it was built in 1908. Sold for a cool $1.3 million in 2021, 'The *Training Day* House' as it's become known is a prime example of Craftsman architecture and includes three bedrooms and three bathrooms in its 1700 sq.ft layout. The use of this house in *Training Day* throws into question the old proverb that crime doesn't pay. The swanky home of ex-cop turned drug dealer, Roger (Scott Glenn), 1031 Everett Street is visually symbolic, sitting in stark contrast to the South Central streets and projects seen elsewhere in *Training Day*, thereby highlighting both that no straight officer of the law or those lower down the pecking order of the narcotics world could afford such a residence. First seen during an ostensibly friendly visit by rogue narcotics officer, Alonzo Harris (Denzel Washington), and rookie cop Jake Hoyt (Ethan Hawke), the house later bears witness to Roger's murder by Alonzo, in a duplicitous act that positions Jake as the fall-guy for Alonzo's corrupt machinations. In the immediate aftermath of Roger's murder, it is viewed from the air and then at ground level as emergency vehicles descend on the scene, with the incident framed as a legitimate operation, Alonzo let's Jake know that if he talks, he won't be believed, and his cards will be marked. Looking down on the city before him, Jake is acutely aware of how the situation and the city itself could swallow him up. **↦Neil Mitchell**

*Directed by Antoine Fuqua*
*Scene description: The aftermath of Roger's murder*
*Timecode for scene: 1:12:05 – 1:17:10*

# PUNCH-DRUNK LOVE (2002)

*Eckhart Auto Body, 10101 Canoga Avenue, Chatsworth*

**OF ALL THE SERENDIPITOUS** characters to have emerged from Paul Thomas Anderson's filmic universe, Barry (Adam Sandler) and Lena (Emily Watson) are the most oddly liberating, refreshingly unpredictable and idiosyncratic of them all. Barry Egan is a small business owner with a short temper, seven overbearing sisters and 'four blonde brothers' (not his own) out to get him after Barry falls victim to a phone sex scam. But he is also a guy who finally starts to get in tune with himself when he inexplicably attracts the affections of a mysterious woman. One morning when he's at work hours before other staff arrive, he steps out of his office and sees a harmonium being abruptly dropped in the street. Not long after, a white car enters the parking lot and a woman in red (Lena) steps out, leaving the car keys with him until the mechanic's shop next door opens. She then disappears around the corner. It's the corner of Eckhart Auto Body, on Canoga Avenue, Chatsworth and is the featured location used in the film as Barry's sparse workspace. The auto body shop still stands today, making for a recognizable spot in the area. Its parking lot even served as a location for a screening of *Punch-Drunk Love* in 2021 as part of the 'Movies on Location' project. The location's realism is in such stark contrast to everything else that happens in those opening frames – from Barry's bright blue suit to the harmonium and Lena's appearance – that it can easily serve as foreshadowing for unfolding events: the surreal, delirious feeling of a new romance. Falling in love is what happens in life, but true love embraces the accidental and only feels real when the possibility of incomprehension is accepted as an essential part of it. Punch-drunk love. **➔ Ada Pîrvu**

*Directed by Paul Thomas Anderson*
*Scene description: A harmonium is dropped in the street*
*Timecode of scene: 0:00:39 – 0:10:09*

# KERB CRAWLERS

Text by THOMAS M. PUHR

## *Nobody Walks in LA*

**EVERYONE KNOWS** you need a car to get around Los Angeles (LA). It is, after all, a so-called 'driving city'. 'Freeways have become so thoroughly ingrained in the civic mentality and vocabulary of Los Angeles', writes Tom Zoellner, 'that they seem like the ocean, the mountains, and the basin – arisen intact; always ready; always relevant; a timeless patrimony of light gray slabs.' If these dizzyingly interconnected roads are considered as fundamental to the city's operation as the elements themselves, then what happens when you have no means of transportation? How do you walk the unwalkable? Highways do much more than take people places; they also bring people closer together, sometimes uncomfortably so. And while it may seem blasphemous to suggest a traffic jam is anything besides hell on earth (think Michael Douglas ditching his gridlocked car at the beginning of *Falling Down*, 1993), there's an undeniable humanity to the whole thing. A nightmarishly congested LA freeway is still less daunting than a miles-long solitary trek through the concrete jungle. You may be a lot of things when stuck in traffic, but one thing you certainly aren't is alone.

Perhaps the odd intimacy behind this most public of spaces explains why some LA-based narratives yank their protagonists from their cars and push them into the great unknown. Severed from an infrastructure's theoretical efficiency, these characters are isolated, unstable and unsure. They don't know where they're going, both literally and figuratively. A walker in a city of drivers is the rudderless wanderer incarnate.

Such is the case with Roger Greenberg (Ben Stiller), the misanthropic protagonist of Noah Baumbach's 2010 romantic comedy. Despite his observation that LA is 'a car culture if ever there was one', both he and his eventual love interest, Florence (Greta Gerwig), do a lot of walking, the latter as early as the opening shot: a slow pan across sunny hilltops that rests on her hiking with the Greenberg family dog, Mahler. Because Greenberg doesn't drive (and maybe can't, due to his recent stay in a mental hospital), he finds himself borrowing rides from Florence, who works as his brother's assistant.

While his carlessness is sometimes mined for laughs – 'Am I gonna drive you to take me?' Florence asks, when he offers her a lift to a doctor's appointment – Greenberg's lone walks around LA primarily emphasize his (mostly self-imposed) alienation. After the one-two punch of being rejected by both his ex-girlfriend Beth (Jennifer Jason Leigh) and reluctant friend Ivan (Rhys Ifans), Greenberg walks home from grocery shopping; arms wrapped around two stuffed paper bags, he navigates the concrete meridian separating lanes of traffic. 'I don't want to be asking anyone for a ride anymore ever', he shouts at Ivan. 'I just turned 41, I should be able to drive.' This throwaway line encapsulates *Greenberg*'s central conflict: here is a man unwilling to acknowledge the help he so clearly needs. It's tough to walk in LA, best to accept a ride (and companionship, and love) when offered.

Though vastly different in style, purpose

is surely Lynch's most labyrinthine dreamscape. And it's Rita's nocturnal wanderings that initiate this phantasmagoric exploration of the human psyche's darkest corners.

Whereas *Mulholland Drive*'s noir influences are a visual foundation upon which Lynch constructs his surreal world, those of David Robert Mitchell's *Under the Silver Lake* (2018) draw more explicitly from their forebears' complex narrative structures. The writer-director's protagonist, Sam (Andrew Garfield), encounters a rogues' gallery of California oddballs in his quest to find a missing blonde, Sarah (Riley Keough); a reclusive comic book artist; members of the alt-rock band Jesus and the Brides of Dracula; a knife-wielding serial killer who wears an owl mask (and nothing else); and a commune of super-rich cultists who bury themselves alive in hopes of ascending to a better world. And there's plenty more where that came from.

Sam's journey is quickly complicated when his Mustang gets towed and he has to continue the investigation on foot; 'I like my car', he breathlessly tells a friend, after trudging up a sloping hill. But it's another such walk that ultimately helps Sam untangle Mitchell's complex mystery. Keeping in mind an acquaintance's esoteric advice – 'If you ever find yourself alone with a coyote, you don't run away. You follow it, see where he takes you' – Sam trails one he sees rummaging through some garbage to a faraway, high-class party. There he will meet the woman who holds the key to finding Sarah. And this epiphany couldn't have come at a better time, as Sam grapples with the dawning awareness that the things to which he has attached so much importance in life – music, art, comics, film – have been carefully orchestrated and delivered by a vast, unfeeling cabal of conspiracists.

Thanks to unprecedented gas prices in the United States, the days of cruising around ala *Dazed and Confused* (1995) are largely gone. Alas, aimless city wandering has been relegated to those on foot, and what connects these films' disparate protagonists is the fact that they must first get lost in order to find themselves. Having no access to a car forces them to slow down, to think. Walking in a city of drivers becomes a means for them to begin their journeys toward something resembling clarity, if not peace. After all, the coyote doesn't take you where you want to be, but where you need to be. ✲

and temperament, David Lynch's *Mulholland Drive* (2001) similarly tosses its protagonist into a carless situation, this time on the titular 50-mile stretch of incomplete road that terminates at the Leo Carrillo State Beach. A quick Google search will tell you Mulholland Drive is not especially welcoming to those on foot – stretches of it have no sidewalk – but this is precisely what Rita (Laura Harring) ends up doing in the film's opening minutes. After barely surviving an assassination attempt – if not for a group of drag-racing teens who crash headfirst into her limousine, she would have been shot by her nameless driver – she stumbles out of the smoking wreck and into the night. Emerging from some bushes, she passes Franklin Ave. and turns onto none other than Sunset Boulevard. It's on this street that Rita will meet aspiring starlet Betty (Naomi Watts), her eventual partner in crime and lover.

'Could be someone's missing, maybe', a detective examining Rita's accident site suggests. He's right in more ways than one, it turns out, as post-crash Rita ostensibly suffers from amnesia (though this 'explanation' crumbles in the face of Lynch's exploration of the inexplicable). 'There was an accident. I came here', she tells Betty, when the latter first walks in on her showering. Even a long sleep fails to jostle her memory. 'I don't know what my name is', she says through tears. 'I don't know who I am.' Thus begins their feverish journey through what

# A walker in a city of drivers is the rudderless wanderer incarnate.

# LOS ANGELES LOCATIONS

## SCENES 33-41

# GREENBERG (2010)

LOCATION *Musso & Frank Grill, 6667 Hollywood Boulevard, Hollywood*

**ROGER GREENBERG** is a fairly unlikeable man. He's irritated by other people's happiness and does everything he can to remain in a constant state of disappointed misery. Noah Baumbach's film sees our feckless hero temporarily returning to Los Angeles to take care of his brother's house and dog while the family holiday in Vietnam, but Roger is as incapable of taking care of other people's stuff as he is at taking care of himself – having recently been discharged from a psychiatric hospital. In steps Florence (Greta Gerwig), a PA to Roger's brother who will be called on for help in managing the day-to-day and become Roger's love interest against her better judgement. Idling his days by building a doghouse, writing disgruntled letters of complaint to random businesses and running errands on foot as he doesn't drive, Roger is at a standstill in his life. His visit to an old friend's party and encounter with an ex-girlfriend only cement his feeling of failure, both having their own grievances about his prior selfish behaviour. Florence affords Roger a chance at renewal and so, while having a muted birthday lunch with his friend Ivan (Rhys Ifans) at Musso & Frank Grill, he calls and invites Florence to join them. Things quickly turn sour however when the restaurant's staff present the birthday boy with a candle-topped desert; the unwanted attention turning Roger's seething anger towards Ivan before he storms out in a huff. The opulent surroundings of Musso & Frank – an iconic Hollywood landmark which has appeared in numerous films – is lost on a man reluctant to embrace the life he never planned on, blinding him to the beauty of the places and the people all around him. **⟿ Gabriel Solomons**

*irected by Noah Baumbach*
*cene description: A birthday party to forget*
*imecode of scene: 0:41:30 – 0:47:08*

# BEGINNERS (2010)

*The Lovell House, 4616 Dundee Drive, Los Feliz*

**A FEW YEARS** after the Spanish Flu of 1918, 'naturopath' Dr Philip Lovel and his wife Leah contacted and commissioned architect Richard Neutra to build a house with health healing properties in the Los Feliz Hills. The Lovell Health House, as it is known, is an iconic, early example of the 'Southern California lifestyle' with walls of glass, no boundaries, no barriers, no secrets. And here in lies director Mike Mills's intriguing choice of using it as a character in his semi-autobiographical film *Beginners*. Through the film's flashbacks and forwards we learn that the parents, Georgia (Mary Page Keller) and Hal (Christopher Plummer) are living 'constructed' lives, for reasons partially explained by Mills's inspired collages of colourful 1950s ideals. Georgia is living a passionless life with a closeted husband who she hoped to 'fix' while Hal explains to his son Oliver (Ewan McGregor) that 'She proposed to me' and 'I liked my life, the museum, our house', 'I thought, "Oh God, I'll try anything"'. Needless to say, Oliver's sense of self suffers. But we soon find that after Georgia's death, Hal exuberantly embraces his long closeted homosexuality without a trace of transitional awkwardness and finds love and community. On this journey, all told with great humour and courage, Hal becomes a lesson to his son. Strangely, the use of the Lovell House may not register with a film audience as there's only a glimpse of its exterior, but as a back story, the house must surely have been alive to the actors and director, 'health' resonating with the chances taken when making new beginnings, and the Lovell House's eternal modernity remains full of that promise. **↠Sandy Reynolds-Wasco and David Wasco**

*irected by Mike Mills*

*cene description: An ailing father rationalizes the masking of his homosexuality*
*imecode for scene: 1:10:50 – 1:13:08*

# SOMEWHERE (2010)

LOCATION *Chateau Marmont, 8221 Sunset Boulevard, Sunset Strip*

**THE CHATEAU MARMONT** has long been associated with Hollywood opulence (and decadence). Modelled off the Château d'Amboise, a castle in central France, the luxury hotel first opened its doors in 1929 as a short-lived apartment complex. The stories associated with the whitewashed, cupola-adorned building range from the superficially comic (Lindsay Lohan's exorbitant bill is the stuff of tabloid legend) to the tragic (John Belushi died from an overdose in one of the hotel's private bungalows). It's only fitting that A-list actor Johnny Marco (sensitively played by Stephen Dorff), the ennui-suffering antihero of Sofia Coppola's *Somewhere*, calls the place home. Any illusions of domesticity are promptly deflated when an uncredited Benicio Del Toro reveals he 'met Bono in 59', Johnny's current room. 59 is not Johnny's room but simply a room: one of the many vague spaces to which the film's title may refer. But this sterile anonymity disappears when Johnny and his 11-year-old daughter Cleo enjoy the hotel grounds together. To the tune of The Strokes' 'I'll Try Anything Once', they play table tennis, take a dip and lounge poolside. The latter shot begins in close-up, slowly pulling back from the father and daughter. They at first seem to be in their own little world, but as the frame expands other patrons enter the scene. They're not really alone, the juxtaposition established by this slow zoom tells us, but they may as well be. This simple moment crystallizes *Somewhere*'s underlying message about home: It's not a matter of where you are, but who you're with. A loved one can make all the difference between somewhere and nowhere. ⟿ *Thomas M. Puhr*

rected by Sofia Coppola
ene description: A father and daughter bond in the heart of Hollywood opulence
mecode for scene: 1:12:50 – 1:15:22

# A BETTER LIFE (2011)

*Wattles Mansion, 1824 N. Curson Avenue, Hollywood Hills*

**'YOU AIN'T JUST BUYIN' A TRUCK, OR A BUSINESS'**, Blasco tells Carlos in *A Better Life*: 'What you're buyin' is the American Dream.' These words inspire Carlos (Demián Bichir) – an undocumented worker – to put all his savings into purchasing the truck from his boss and starting his own gardening business. But this dream is promptly yanked out from under him when a man he hires steals his truck during their first day on the job. That this heart-wrenching scene takes place at Wattles Mansion only highlights the extreme disparity between Carlos's aspirations and lived experiences, between the Hollywood elite and the working class communities of East Los Angeles. Erected in 1907 and credited with helping put turn-of-the-century LA on the map, the mansion and its surrounding gardens provide an ironic backdrop to Carlos's struggle to achieve the titular 'better life'. That the mansion's original owner, banker Gurdon Wattles, was vehemently anti-union, or that the property's surrounding gardens were modelled in part on Mexican landscapes may very well have factored into the location's inclusion in the film. Admiring a beautiful view of the city from high up in a palm tree he's trimming, Carlos spots his new hire, Santiago, running to the parked truck. The mansion's bright, imposing façade (used most recently as the home of James McKay [Tobey Maguire] in *Babylon*, 2023) looms over Carlos as he races down the tree and through the front yard, helplessly watching his truck (and dreams) disappear down the road. Director Chris Weitz's 2011 reworking of *Bicycle Thieves* offers a sensitive, empathetic portrait of a man whose modest goals – more than anything, he just wants his son to go to a nicer high school – are met with roadblock after roadblock, but whose honesty and fatherly love see him through. ◆ *Thomas M. Puhr*

*rected by Chris Weitz*
*ene description: A man's truck, and dreams, are ripped away*
*mecode for scene: 0:36:45 – 0:39:55*

# RAMPART (2011)

**THE LAPD'S CRASH** (Community Resources against Street Hoodlums) unit was tasked with curbing gang-related crime in the city of Los Angeles from the late 1970s until 2000, when it was dissolved due to some of the most egregious acts of police corruption the city had ever seen. CRASH had a presence within all LAPD patrol divisions, but none was more infamous than the CRASH unit based out of the Rampart station, which closed in 2008 and relocated about two miles away. Serving areas to the west of Downtown LA, Rampart has been either directly portrayed or alluded to on screen in films like *Colors* (Hopper 1988) and *Training Day* (Fuqua 2001). Both films are set in the eras in which they were made. *Rampart*, however, is a period piece, made twelve years after the events it portrays. Set in 1999, the film follows David Brown (Woody Harrelson), a corrupt renegade officer based out of the Rampart division whose individual actions mirror violent and disturbing abuses of CRASH officers of the era, though he's not assigned to CRASH. The original Rampart station, which today houses units including SWAT and K-9, was built in 1966. Staying true to Rampart's mid-century modern aesthetic, the station was recreated for the film only five minutes away from the original building. As David enters the station, protests presumably against CRASH are heard in the background. The floating camera gets a good look at the 1965 structure both inside and out.
•➠*Jared Cowan*

*irected by Oren Moverman*
*scene description: Rampart inside and out*
*imecode for scene: 0:20:40 – 0:21:57*

# END OF WATCH (2012)

LOCATION *Alleyway, West side of Compton Avenue between 48th Place and 49th Street, Central-Alameda*

**AT THE END OF 1996,** the cramped and crumbling Newton Division, the LAPD's oldest surviving station, was set to close. In a month's time, the officers based out of Newton – serving areas of Downtown Los Angeles and South LA – were set to move into a new $17 million, two-storey building. According to the *Los Angeles Times*, the precinct was 'under pressure to improve its relationship with citizens' (*It's a Dump They're Going to Miss* Emily Otani, 29 November 1996). David Ayer's frenetic police drama asks if it's possible to build positive public relations within a disenfranchised and disparaged community – this one dubbed 'Shootin' Newton' by the officers who work the beat – where gangs and cops are constantly at war with each other. Ayer's film was largely shot in and around the Newton Division service area, including the real, new-and-improved police station. Over the course of 105 minutes of dash cam, body cam and personal camcorder footage, we're deeply immersed in the private and professional lives of two decorated officers, Brian Taylor (Jake Gyllenhaal) and Mike Zavala (Michael Peña), who are more like brothers than colleagues. Through coincidence, curiosity and perseverance, Taylor and Zavala make arrests and disturbing discoveries that incur the wrath of a Mexican drug cartel and a local gang that works on the cartel's behalf. With targets on their backs, Taylor and Zavala are ambushed in a frenzied assassination attempt that forces them to escape into a dark, narrow alleyway where one of the officer's lives is devastatingly extinguished. **↝Jared Cowan**

rected by David Ayer

ene description: An officer shooting turns a dark alleyway into hallowed ground
mecode for scene: 1:29:52 – 1:36:04

# NIGHTCRAWLER (2014)

**IN NATURE,** vultures can be found feeding on the dead and dying and thus gain life at the expense of others. Leonard 'Leo' Bloom (Jake Gyllenhaal) is just such a scavenger in Dan Gilroy's gritty thriller about a petty thief turned freelance photojournalist who sells footage of graphic incidents to local TV stations; occasionally tampering with crime scenes to get the best results. Ruthlessly ambitious but lacking the moral compass necessary to know when lines have been crossed, Leonard will resort to sabotage, blackmail and even murder to get what he wants. Earlier in the film, after he's pawned a stolen bike in order to buy a camcorder and police radio scanner, Leo decides to hire an assistant desperate enough for money and dumb enough not to ask questions. The interview with doe-eyed Rick (Riz Ahmed) takes place at Dinah's Family Restaurant, Leo seating himself at the distinctive curved window with a prominent view of the busy streets outside. With his intense stare, upright posture and mid-management rhetoric, Leo presents himself as the success story he so wishes to appear, having mastered the confident sales schtick with which many associate the attainment of a certain kind of American Dream. The homeless Rick simply wants a paying gig, and it'll be his naivety, paired with Rick's disregard for anyone who gets in his way that will prove disastrous later down the line. Sadly, like so many of Los Angeles' historic diners, Dinah's closed up shop at the original location after 64 years in business due to a new development along Sepulveda Boulevard, and has since relocated to Culver City. ⤳ *Gabriel Solomons*

irected by Dan Gilroy
ene description: Leonard recruits Rick
mecode for scene: 0:23:30 – 0:26:35

# DOPE (2015)

*Thurgood Marshall Justice Plaza bridge, 1 E. Regent Street, Inglewood*

**OF ALL THE LOCATIONS** utilized in Rick Famuyiwa's sharp and vibrant coming-of-age drama, *Dope*, the bridge that crosses Regent Street bearing the inscription Thurgood Marshall Justice Plaza is the most culturally and politically significant. Thurgood Marshall's standing as the first African American Supreme Court judge is memorialized across the United States, and the plaza in LA afforded writer-director Famuyiwa the opportunity to visually compliment the themes that underpin *Dope*'s pointed social commentary. Marshall's quote that 'the Justice system can force open doors and sometimes even knock down walls. But it cannot build bridges. That job belongs to you and me' reverberates throughout *Dope*. A tale of aspirations and expectations, stereotypes and mould-breaking and the pathways our environments offer or deny, *Dope* focuses on Malcolm Adekambi (Shameik Moore), a 1990s hip hop loving straight A student from Inglewood, his geeky friends and the potentially life-derailing street crime they inadvertently find themselves caught up in. After being briefly spotted during an earlier chase sequence, the Thurgood Marshall Justice Plaza bridge becomes more integral to *Dope*'s narrative towards the end of the movie. Having expertly manipulated the perilously stacked cards to his advantage, Malcolm finally sits down to write his personal statement to accompany his application for Harvard University. Through a combination of direct-to-camera address, voice over and montage, Malcolm's impassioned statement addresses the racial stereotypes and inequalities African Americans still sadly experience to this day. It is the shots of Malcolm standing below the Thurgood Marshall Justice Plaza bridge that hammer home the facts that opportunities exist but accessing them is littered with systemic pitfalls and ingrained prejudices for large swathes of the population. **•» Neil Mitchell**

*Directed by Rick Famuyiwa*
*Scene description: Malcolm writes his personal statement for Harvard*
*Timecode for scene: 1:27:35 – 1:30:10*

# TANGERINE (2015)

LOCATION 'Donut Time', 6785 Santa Monica Boulevard, Hollywood

**SEAN BAKER'S LO-FI COMEDY** about a transvestite prostitute on the hunt for her cheating pimp/boyfriend on Christmas Eve, is best remembered for having been entirely filmed using an iPhone camera; a technique that lends a grungy, realistic tone to this small but perfectly formed story of friendship, betrayal and disappointment. Taking place over the course of a single afternoon and evening, Sin-Dee's (Kitana Kiki Rodriguez) frenetic search through the streets of Los Angeles is kickstarted when her friend Alexandra (Mya Taylor) let's slip about Chester's (James Ransone) philandering while sharing a rainbow-sprinkled donut at Donut Time, and it's where the closing scenes of the film take place as random characters converge for a rousing finale. Having located the girl who Chester's been sleeping with, Sin-Dee confronts him at the 24-hour eatery but they are soon joined by Ramzik (Karren Karagulian); an Armenian cab driver (with a weakness for trans prostitutes), his disapproving mother-in-law and Ramzik's wife, all of who's story has been running in parallel to Sin-Dee and Alexandra's throughout. Movies are full of evocative locations, and the best are themselves characters that help in telling a story. Donut Time, which sadly closed its doors in 2016, had long been home to a vibrant community of trans women who made a living on the streets nearby, and its use lent an authenticity to Baker's film which would have been hard to replicate elsewhere. It's modesty as a location was also in keeping with Baker's everyday tale of struggle on the streets of LA; a city that often resembles a donut: showy, sweet but a little sickly. The location, now painted bright pink, is home to Trejo's Coffee and Donuts which was opened in 2017 by LA native and iconic movie strongman Danny Trejo. **⇥ Gabriel Solomons**

*Directed by Sean Baker*
*Scene description: All hell breaks loose at Donut Time*
*Timecode for scene: 0:58:15 – 1:15:35*

# HOLLYWOOD'S BACKYARD

## *The San Fernando Valley Onscreen*

Text by
ANDREW
NOCK

**FOR MOVIEGOERS** of a certain generation, whether they know it or not, the San Fernando Valley represents the playground for their coming-of-age fantasies. A sun bleached, suburban canvas for stories of teens finding their way in life and love. For good reason, the San Fernando Valley has been called 'America's Suburb'. *Fast Times at Ridgemont High* (1982), *E.T. the Extra-Terrestrial* (1982), *The Karate Kid* (1984), *Back to the Future* (1985) and, of course, *Valley Girl* (1983) represented an idealized America of palm trees, malls, pretty people, swimming pools and perpetual sunshine for filmgoers all over the world – including me. I grew up in the north of England during the 1970s and 1980s. Steeped in ancient history, the towns seemed drab and frozen in time. There were no miner's strikes or Yorkshire Rippers in the lives of these American characters dressed in florescent spandex, headbands and high-top sneakers. Their modern homes

and wide boulevards were dream-like, aspirational, yet seemingly attainable.

Today, I have been filming in Los Angeles for over twenty years and have lived in the Valley for over ten. Almost every day I drive around on errands and see iconic Valley film locations like *The Karate Kid*'s South Seas Apartments, where Elvis filled up his 1959 Stingray in *Clambake* (1967). I've had lunch at The Great Wall restaurant – which sadly closed in 2023 – from *Drive* (2011), before cruising past the Reseda Theater from *Boogie Nights* (1997) and the house of horrors within Maynard's Pawn Shop from *Pulp Fiction* (1994), to end up meeting friends for cocktails in the red leather booth at Casa Vega where Brad Pitt and Leo DiCaprio got drunk in *Once Upon Time in Hollywood* (2019). It may not be the most glamorous place, but filmmakers who live in LA see its incredible, versatile value. The Valley is Hollywood's backyard.

Although 'the Valley' has always gotten a bad rap from residents of other parts of LA – it's too hot, boring or a cultural wasteland – its ability to stand in for 'anywhere USA' made it perfect for filmmakers since the industry's earliest days. It hasn't hurt that the Valley is a more affordable home to studios like Warner Bros, Universal and Disney, dozens of independent production companies, thousands of actors, writers, composers producers and crew members than the other side of the Hollywood Hills.

The Valley is a vast, sprawling grid of 34 neighbourhoods stretching 260 square miles and home to around 1.8 million people. The eastern border of the Valley features the Verdugo Mountains and the city of Burbank

long-running *Lone Ranger* series (1945–57), but the most infamous one here was the Spahn Movie Ranch in Chatsworth. This 55-acre property was once the site of King Vidor's psychological western *Duel in the Sun* (1946), but by 1968 had become the headquarters of Charles Manson's 'Family' who planned their murderous spree against Hollywood elite the following year. Spahn Ranch, and members of the 'Family', can be seen in two productions: *The Other Side of Madness* (1971), and the Academy Award-nominated documentary *Manson* (1973). For Quentin Tarantino's *Once Upon a Time in Hollywood* (2019), Spahn Ranch was recreated on the site of the old Corriganville Ranch, now a regional park in Simi Valley. The infamy of the Manson Family was not the only thing that scared off major productions. By the late 1960s, westerns had fallen out of favour, and the new 118 freeway construction caused so much noise that filmmakers headed further north. However, the Valley still had much more to offer filmmakers than doubling for Utah or Mars. It was time to celebrate itself.

For decades, Van Nuys Boulevard has been the centre of the Valley's obsession with car culture – especially American muscle cars. In the 1970s, Van Nuys Blvd was the place for teens to cruise and show off their Pontiacs and Mustangs. Producers tried to cash in on the cruising scene with the teen comedies *Corvette Summer* (1978) and *Van Nuys Blvd.* (1979) – one of the first films about life in the Valley and not a double for elsewhere.

Since the 1990s, one local filmmaker, above all, has put a spotlight on the Valley – Paul Thomas Anderson. *Boogie Nights*, *Magnolia* (1999), *Punch-Drunk Love* (2002) and *Licorice Pizza* (2021) have been called love letters to the Valley celebrating its people, dive bars, 1970s wood panelled restaurants, motels and locally owned stores – complete with quirky signage. Finally, we have a master filmmaker playing the Valley for itself, and all it has to offer.

Over the last 30 years, the Valley's demographics have been changing with a huge increase in Latinx residents and almost 40 per cent of its residents are foreign born, like me. There will be new stories to tell, through a new lens, inspired by everything the Valley has to offer a new generation of filmmakers. ❖

– home to Warner Bros and Disney Studios. The eastern side of the Valley was important back at the dawn of silent cinema. In 1912, it became the site to a massive ranch owned by Hollywood pioneer D. W. Griffith. In the same year, Universal Studios purchased a ranch to the south – later known as Laskey Ranch. Somewhere between the two ranches, Griffith staged the massive Civil War battle in his landmark, and controversial, film *Birth of a Nation* (1915). It has been called the first blockbuster Hollywood hit. Today the location is home to Forest Lawn Cemetery, the resting place of such stars as Buster Keaton, Bette Davis and Carrie Fisher.

The western side of the Valley is in the impressive shadow of the Santa Susana Mountains and Simi Hills. Its rugged sandstone bluffs have inspired directors and location scouts to use them as alien worlds, Corsican villages, Mexican villages, and, of course, western landscapes. Several movie ranches were located here. The most famous being the Iverson Ranch that staged scenes for thousands of productions including John Ford's classic *Stagecoach* (1939), Laurel and Hardy's *The Flying Deuces* (1939), the Republic serials of the 1940s and 1950s and the

Although 'the Valley' has always gotten a bad rap from residents of other parts of LA, its ability to stand in for 'anywhere USA' made it perfect for filmmakers since the industry's earliest days.

# LOS ANGELES LOCATIONS

## SCENES 42-50

# LA LA LAND (2016)

*Ramp connecting Interstates 105 and 110, South Los Angeles*

**MUNDANE REALITY** gives way to Technicolor movie magic in the opening number to Damien Chazelle's *La La Land*. The first thing we see after a narrow black-and-white aspect ratio expands into glorious CinemaScope is a clear blue sky. Honking horns and blaring radios undercut this serene image. 'It's another hot, sunny day here in Southern California', a radio DJ announces. The camera then tilts down to gridlocked traffic on the ramp connecting Interstates 105 and 110. However, every driver's worst nightmare morphs into a dance studio when singing commuters explode from their cars and onto the road. A four-piece band emerges from the back of a delivery truck; skateboarders and bicyclists use car hoods as makeshift ramps; and, in a feat of musical coordination, car roofs become a shared dancefloor for roughly 100 perfectly synchronized performers. It's an exhilarating moment, one which captures both what draws so many aspiring artists to Los Angeles and what makes the experience of seeing a film on the big screen so special. The accompanying lyrics to 'Another Day of Sun' reinforce this love for the collective dream that is Hollywood: 'Climb these hills, I'm reaching for the heights. And chasing all the lights that shine', the primary colour-clad commuters sing. The ramp – which was constructed in 1993 – turns out to be an ideal spot for such hopeful lines, as it offers a breathtaking view of the downtown area. But the dream, alas, can't last forever; the music ends, everyone returns to their cars, and the din of traffic resumes on that slab of concrete. For a few precious minutes, though, everything is sunny.
**➼ Thomas M. Puhr**

Photo © 2014 Robert Foulkes

*Directed by Damien Chazelle*
*Scene description: A traffic jam transforms into a dance party*
*Timecode for scene: 0:00:00 – 0:04:47*

# THE NEON DEMON (2016)

*The Pasada Motel, 3625 E. Colorado Boulevard, Pasadena*

**LIKE LOS ANGELES** and its Hollywood movie machine, motels and models both deal in the illusory. Room 212 in the Pasada Motel, offers an ersatz home for Jessie (Elle Fanning) – orphan, model and a girl who has *it*. 'That whole deer in the headlights thing is exactly what they want' says Ruby (Jenna Malone), gazing at our heroine in a dressing room mirror as though she could drink in her beauty with a look. Jessie's yet to acquire her hard gaze and battle-scarred smile, and her lack thereof is, indeed, exactly what 'they' want: photographers and models alike covet her youth like a choice morsel. We first enter 212 to watch Jessie preparing for a shoot. Seen through honeyed sunlight, she's a vision of purity, dressed in white, in a room decorated in pastel florals and charmingly mismatched furniture. This could almost be a teenage girl's bedroom, and it feels as cosy as a cocoon after neon-lit studios and bars. But looks can be deceiving. Fluorescent strip lights and traffic thundering along the Foothill Freeway outside reminds us this motel isn't home – and sooner or later, Jessie will need to emerge. Things are already forcing their way in. A very real cougar prowls her darkened room. Will Jessie be devoured? Or perhaps this portents a predatory shift for our young heroine. After a sojourn with the eponymous demon on a runway, she returns to the motel, ready for her final transformation. And none too soon – the outside is invading, expelling her in the process. Screams drift in from next door, and in a moment with notes of *Repulsion* (1965) walls become malleable with reaching hands. The doorknob rattles: danger. Jessie leaves room 212 and steps out into the night. But what is she? And who will be eating whom? **↝ Georgina Guthrie**

*Directed by Nicolas Winding Refn*
*Scene description: You can check out but you can never leave ...*
*Timecode for scene: 0:20:11 – 0:30:34 and 1:09:27 – 1:17:26*

# DESTROYER (2018)

LOCATION *Victory Memorial Grove, 1350 Elysian Park Drive, Echo Park*

**WHILE KARYN KUSAMA'S** *Destroyer* is best remembered for Nicole Kidman's physical transformation as a hollowed out detective wrestling with a guilty conscience, it is also one of the best recent examples of a film to use interesting Los Angeles locations seldom seen onscreen. Detective Erin Bell is a walking zombie, having lapsed into self-destruct mode following a botched robbery sixteen years prior while working undercover. With the discovery that the robbery's gang leader Silas (Toby Kebbell) has resurfaced, Bell is set on tracking him down and exacting revenge for his killing of her undercover FBI partner and lover Chris (Sebastian Stan) with whom she also had a baby. Her shake-down of remaining gang members with information on Silas's whereabouts takes us on a gritty tour of the city that includes the Victory Memorial Grove, a leafy woodland with trees planted to commemorate lives lost in WWI, and which overlooks Dodger Stadium. It's here that Erin chases and catches up with Arturo, a member of the gang atoning for his past crimes by offering pro bono legal services to immigrants in a nearby church. Exhausted and out of breath after a scramble up to the hill's summit, Arturo provides Bell with the location of another of Silas's accomplices as the two wonder 'when it all adds up to even'; both of them painfully aware of the past crimes they are trying, and failing, to bury. ➼ *Gabriel Solomons*

*Directed by Karyn Kusama*
**Scene description: Detective Erin Bell chases Arturo into Victory Memorial Grove**
**Timecode for scene: 0:36:45 – 0:40:15**

# UNDER THE SILVER LAKE (2018)

LOCATION *Bronson Caves, 3200 Canyon Drive, Griffith Park*

**WHEN WINSTON CHURCHILL** referred to the covert ambitions of Russia in 1939 as 'a riddle, wrapped in a mystery, inside an enigma', he could just as easily be describing David Mitchell's puzzling 2018 neo-noir whodunnit *Under the Silver Lake* – a film that revels in throwing the audience off balance every time they tentatively find their feet. Centred around the paranoid antics of LA slacker Sam (Andrew Garfield), who's brief encounter with the beautiful Sarah (Riley Keough) leads to a frazzled city-wide search after she goes missing from their Silver Lake apartment complex, the movie unravels like a psychedelic retelling of *The Wizard of Oz* (1939) via *Rear Window* (1954) and *The Long Goodbye* (1973). Convinced that there are secret codes everywhere which will help him solve Sarah's disappearance, Sam's antics are conducted through a haze of drugs, sex and booze as his journey takes him down a nightmarish rabbit hole below Tinseltown's glitzy façade. Midway through the film, our amateur gumshoe attends a party at Hollywood Forever Cemetery, where he meets the mysterious balloon girl. Rebuffing his line of questioning, the girl leads Sam down into the aptly named Crypt Club, where after some frisky banter, the pair take to the dancefloor upon hearing R.E.M's 'What's the Frequency, Kenneth'. The song's use – inspired as it was by William Tager's attack of the CBS news anchor Dan Rather in 1986 – offers some hint as to Sam's own role as an unreliable narrator since Tager was convinced the media were beaming signals into his head. The producers used Griffith Park's Bronson Caves, located three miles north of the cemetery and best known as the Batman caves from the 1960s TV show, as the setting to create the Crypt Club – and the ancient caves provide the perfect eerie setting to suggest the threatening underworld from which Sam has descended and will find it hard to escape. **•• Gabriel Solomons**

*Directed by David Robert Mitchell*
*Scene description: Drug-induced revelry in The Crypt Club*
*Timecode for scene: 0:59:05 – 1:04:00*

# ONCE UPON A TIME IN HOLLYWOOD (2019)

LOCATION *'Van Nuys Drive-In', originally located at 15040 Roscoe Boulevard, Panorama City*

**A BRIEF SCENE** it may be, but the sequence in which Cliff Booth (Brad Pitt) drives to his trailer park home after returning Rick Dalton (Leonardo DiCaprio) to his plush Cielo Drive residence is weighted with meaning both about the characters themselves and the Hollywood movie industry itself. The scene also exemplifies just how impressive Tarantino's recreation of 1960s Los Angeles is, thanks to the shots of the now long-demolished Van Nuys Drive-In on Roscoe Boulevard (and where Vista Middle School now stands). Opened in 1948 with room for 891 cars and one of many drive-ins owned and operated by Pacific Theatres, The Van Nuys Drive-In seen in *Once Upon a Time in Hollywood* is in actuality a combination of the Paramount Drive-In in the Southeast LA region and a miniature recreation of the Van Nuys's famous mural frontage. For Cliff Booth, the Van Nuys Drive-In literally and symbolically dominates his physical and emotional headspace, as Cliff's ramshackle trailer home is situated on a dusty, derelict plot of land right next door. Big screen fantasies and cold, hard realities clash in just over a minute of the movie's running time, with the drive-in's patrons in blissful ignorance to the modest existence of the stunt-double living a stone's throw from where fictional visions of others' lives, times and places play out on a daily basis. Booth lives in the shadows while Dalton, despite his own insecurities and flagging career, enjoys the limelight and the trappings of success. The movie playing at the Van Nuys Drive-In as Cliff Booth arrives home acts as a clear reminder of his, and other stunt workers', unheralded status in the movie industry and among the vast majority of moviegoers. Fun fact: Vista Middle School's mascot, the Vaquero, is a reference to the vaquero that was on the mural of the original Van Nuys Drive-In (as seen opposite) **↝ Neil Mitchell**

*Directed by Quentin Tarantino*
**Scene description: Cliff drives back to his trailer home**
**Timecode for scene: 0:21:08 – 0:22:18**

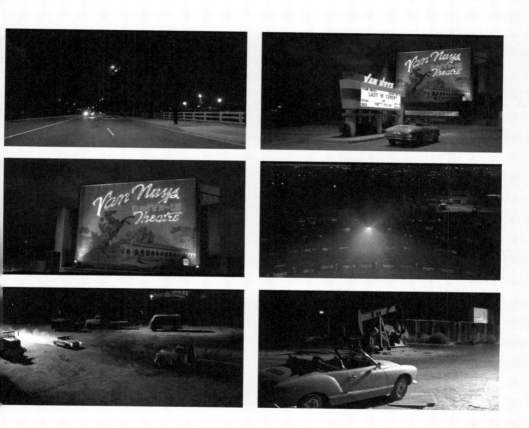

# BOOKSMART (2019)

LOCATION *Lido Pizza, 15232 Victory Boulevard, Van Nuys*

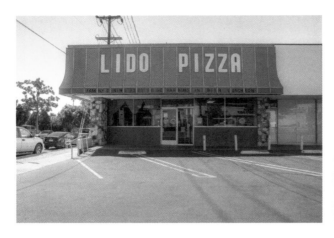

'**HOW MANY ORDERS** that big do you think Lido's could have filled tonight?' Amy asks best friend Molly, as the two watch video footage of a classmate karate-chopping fifteen empty pizza boxes from the beloved Van Nuys restaurant. This detail will finally deliver the duo to the blowout house party they've been seeking, on the eve of their high school graduation. Via a graceful tracking shot, director Olivia Wilde then follows grumbling deliveryman Pat (played to deadpan perfection by Mike O'Brien) from the interior of the restaurant – where glistening, New York-style pizzas are taken out of the oven and boxed – to his car. In one of the film's best visual gags, Amy and Molly – their hair farcically draped over their faces as makeshift masks – pop out from their hiding spot in the backseat and demand to know the address of the night's unusually large order. Pat is willing to help, but not before giving his unexpected guests a good talking-to. 'You're basically children', he scolds them, 'and you just willingly got in the car of a strange man?' Lido's function in the narrative is two-fold, guiding our heroines to the party and setting up a wickedly funny reveal (Pat turns out to be an actual serial killer, a sketch of his face taped to a police bulletin board notifies us). It also embodies that most high school of drunken takeout orders: some good, greasy pizza. Food indeed brings people together, and Amy and Molly's coming of age may have never reached completion if not for that stack of Lido's boxes. ⇥ *Thomas M. Puhr*

Directed by Olivia Wilde
Scene description: 'You just willingly got in the car of a strange man?'
Timecode for scene: 0:48:20 – 0:52:57

# PROMISING YOUNG WOMAN (2020)

*St. Louis Drug Company, 2100 E. 1st Street, Boyle Heights*

**SOMETHING DOESN'T FEEL RIGHT.** Pharmacies don't look like nightclubs, with signage flashing in rainbow neons and Paris Hilton piped over the airwaves. When Ryan (Bo Burnham) sings along to Hilton's 'Stars Are Blind' and the formerly hostile Cassandra (Carey Mulligan) starts grooving along, alarm bells ring. Unapproachable as a cornered cat, Cassie has, up until this point, rebuffed all romantic advances lest they distract her from her one-woman mission to teach men a lesson: Night after night, she gets dolled up, heads to a bar and pretends to be blind drunk. Without fail, a self-proclaimed 'nice guy' swoops in to 'save' her, or in other words, takes the seemingly incapacitated Cassie home to rape her. Cassandra snaps back into icy sobriety at the critical moment, sending her would-be abuser reeling in shock. It's a bitter routine forged from the poison of years-old trauma. The film's confectionery colour palette and sunny suburban Ohio setting form an ironic counterpoint to the film's darker heart. By the time we make it to the pharmacy on 1st St., in LA's historic Boyle Heights neighbourhood, those delicate pastels have morphed into giallo-esque reds and blacks as irony acquires a more sinister flavour. Our smitten couple's boogie round the aisles is all frothy surface; a subversive romcom scene d'amour with danger lurking just out of frame. And the beguiling Ryan? He's as much a part of that illusion as the neon pharmacy sign glaring above them. Don't trust appearances. The film's not even shot in Ohio.
➻ *Georgina Guthrie*

Directed by Emerald Fennell
Scene description: A singalong in the aisles
Timecode for scene: 1:06:37 – 1:08:37

# LICORICE PIZZA (2021)

LOCATION *'Fat Bernie's Pinball Palace', 21758 Devonshire Street, Chatsworth*

**WHETHER PAUL THOMAS ANDERSON** is the only filmmaker interested in recreating the flashy 1970s of his home turf, the San Fernando Valley, or he's the only one who can do it with heart and soul – a likely combination of both – is up for discussion. What's not open for debate is that Anderson was able to once again successfully stitch together the era for his offbeat, haphazard comedy *Licorice Pizza* in a city that isn't particularly known for preserving old buildings. But sometimes it just means looking where no one else bothers to look. After the 1973 Oil Embargo shuts down Fat Bernie's Water Beds – vinyl is partially made from oil – 15-year-old child actor and fledgling entrepreneur Gary Valentine (Cooper Hoffman) finds his next business venture in pinball when the beloved arcade game, previously deemed as gambling, becomes legal again in Los Angeles. Gary converts the waterbed location – found in a period accurate, and largely unchanged, strip of stores in the northwest Valley neighbourhood of Chatsworth – into Fat Bernie's Pinball Palace (the location is right around the corner from *Punch-Drunk Love*'s Eckhart Auto Body). But all of the ambition that has led Gary to the arcade's glittery and successful opening night means little without the presence of his estranged friend Alana (Alana Haim). After Alana's political aspirations come to a screeching halt, the two instinctually find each other on the streets of the Valley, rekindling their friendship and igniting a brewing, idiosyncratic love within the blinding searchlights outside of Fat Bernie's Pinball Palace. **✦ Jared Cowan**

*irected by Paul Thomas Anderson*
*cene description: Alana and Gary find love at Fat Bernie's Pinball Palace*
*imecode for scene: 2:05:28 – 2:06:15*

# BARBIE (2023)

*Windward Plaza and 407 Ocean Front Walk, Venice Beach*

**WHEN 'STEREOTYPICAL'** Barbie's (Margot Robbie) idyllic existence is suddenly thrown off-balance from flat feet and un-Barbie-like thoughts of mortality, she has to leave Barbie Land and travel to the Real World to repair a rift caused by – we're led to believe – a disillusioned girl who has emotionally detached from her childhood Barbie doll. After traversing playful, candy-colored dioramas, Barbie and Ken (Ryan Gosling), decked out in neon rollerblades and fluorescent beachwear, arrive in a sun-drenched and graffiti-covered Venice Beach. Men – some with stunned glares, others with libidinous smirks – look Ken and Barbie up and down. Teenagers flat-out laugh in their faces. The two life-size Mattel dolls aren't privy to whatever joke is in play. When a group of preppy college guys approach and one of them says to Barbie, obnoxiously, "Give us a smile, blondie," it's clear that this is not the same Venice Beach that was home to a real Boardwalk freak show or has been known as a refuge for Bohemians, renegades, outcasts and misfits alike. No, the world that Barbie and Ken have freely skated into is one in which obtuse school bullies, chauvinist CEOs, and far-right American politics have claimed authority. Ken is immediately seduced by the testosterone-filled ocean air while Barbie is left with a feeling of unease, which is only exacerbated when some troglodytic construction workers reduce the linguistically-astute Barbie to nothing more than a pretty face. If only the Real World, United States had taken a cue from Barbie Land and elected a smart, fierce and compassionate woman for president. ↝*Jared Cowan*

*Directed by Greta Gerwig*
**Scene description: Barbie and Ken rollerblade into the Real World**
*Timecode for scene: 0:27:26 – 0:29:27*

# LAPOCALYPSE

Text by
FABRICE
ZIOLKOWSKI

*Los Angeles, The City We Love to Destroy*

**IN HIS MASTERFUL** if at times over-the-top analysis of the destruction of Los Angeles by any means necessary (*Ecology of Fear: Los Angeles and the Imagination of Disaster*, 1998), the recently departed Mike Davis (*City of Quartz: Excavating the Future in Los Angeles*, 1990) explored the myriad fictional methods by which the city has been burned to a crisp, blown away, invaded by zombies or aliens or other evil forms, nuked, shaken to bits and otherwise razed to the ground. It's bad enough in books, but the apparently unquenchable thirst for the annihilation of LA reaches a veritable frenzy when it comes to its portrayal in the movies.

So why does LA get the brunt of all this cinematic mayhem? Is it a wish for the outside world to destroy a place often seen in a negative light – a sort of moral and ultimately heavenly retribution for the area's bad behaviour? Is it simply the fact that the movie industry in an industry town doesn't have to travel far and rejoices in blowing up the Hollywood sign or the Capitol Records building or the iconic City Hall? Or is there some wicked masochistic thrill experienced by ordinary citizens watching freeways buckle under the stress of earth-

quakes or gawping at those damn downtown skyscrapers as they get blown to smithereens? Forget the city of Our Lady of the Angels, welcome to Our Lady of Perpetual Destruction.

Apocalyptic visions are firmly rooted in almost all religions either as a final episode or as an occasional bit of fireworks such as God's destruction of the wicked cities of Sodom and Gomorrah (*Sodom and Gomorrah*, Robert Aldrich 1962). But representations of large cities being wiped away under horrifying circumstances have multiplied exponentially since the discovery of the remains of Pompeii (in the eighteenth century), the Industrial Revolution and the advent of modern warfare referencing either imagined events (London, Paris, New York) or real-life occurrences (Hiroshima, Dresden, Warsaw). Major population centres reduced to piles of rubble. While end-of-times rhetoric has often been used to describe various real-life riots that have ravaged the city, Angelenos have been the victims of fictional eradication in disproportionate numbers compared to other locations around the world – or maybe that's just the way it feels.

Just exactly where the havoc takes place in all these movies can vary. Downtown, Hollywood, the beaches, take your pick. It may be narrowed down to a location such as the Wilshire area in *Miracle Mile* (see separate entry). But the devastation is generally city-wide if not county-wide. Yet it often only serves as hors d'oeuvres of sorts. For the devastation brought upon LA often appears merely as a harbinger of the wider obliteration of California, if not that of the entire country, continent or planet. No city does total destruction better than LA.

The list of films in which LA gets the brunt of it is too long to appear in this modest volume. In any case, the genre is constantly being augmented by new ways filmmakers invent to torture and decimate the Southland. However, it shou

already be clear that these films shouldn't be confused with run-of-the-mill disaster films that do not necessarily involve the obliteration of the city as a whole (*Airport,* 1970, *The Poseidon Adventure,* 1972, *The Towering Inferno,* 1975). The trail to the total eradication is marked with some of the following gems:

### ALIEN INVASION

No doubt it all starts off with *The War of the Worlds* in its 1953 version delocalized from London to LA. Martians attack and destroy much of LA before succumbing to banal human bacteria. See also *Independence Day* (1996), *Battle: Los Angeles* (2011) and *This Is the End* (2013), for a more comedic stab at the genre.

### HUMAN FOLLY

This includes nuclear warfare or accidents (*Kiss Me Deadly,* 1955) and can dovetail into broader repercussions on nature as in *Them* (1954) in which gigantic murderous nuke-mutated ants invade the city's underground sewer system. See also *Panic in Year Zero* (1962) and *Miracle Mile* (1989).

### NATURE

In this category, nature strikes on its own bringing death and havoc by geological (seismic) or climactic events: nature doing what it pleases without giving a good goddamn about those silly humans who have had the dumb idea of building a megalopolis on a major geological fault line. The archetypal film in this category is *Earthquake* (1974). A special growing category includes stories in which the eco-apocalypse is triggered by man-made foolishness.

Nature takes revenge or follows through on the various warnings it has emitted over time as in *The Day after Tomorrow* (2004). See also *Volcano* (1997) and *San Andreas* (2015).

### ZOMBIES

A special mention for the case of zombies brought about by *Night of the Comet* (1984) in which case the invasion of the flesh-eating ghouls is the story itself. See also *This Is the End* in a more comedic approach.

### POST-APOCALYPSE LA'S END TIMES

This isn't really about dystopia. The vision of our future presented in *Blade Runner* (1982) may be dystopic, but it's not post-apocalyptic. When the dust has settled and the smoke from the last fire has cleared, LA stands as a pile of rubble from which emerge any number of horrendous scenarios. A man alone, or at least he thinks he's alone (*Omega Man,* 1972) or a small group trying to survive as best it can, facing various apparently insurmountable obstacles not least of which are zombies (reread earlier paragraph for a continuous loop effect).

The expression 'dancing on the edge of a volcano' was used to describe the political, cultural and social turmoil that enveloped the Weimar Republic before the Nazi takeover in 1933. As one prepares to visit LA, one might wonder if the shit will come down when you just happen to be there for a few days. The worst of luck. As a full-time resident of the city, these visions and the sense of pending doom they engender might make you anxious. But hey, this is LA, so you just shrug it off, get back into your car and head down the freeway for another day of sun.

### CITY HALL COMES DOWN

Unlike the New York skyline, it took LA a relatively long time to have iconic buildings to blow up in an all-out attack by Martians. Inaugurated in 1928 and appearing in various film and television productions for decades, the LA City Hall was based on the Mausoleum of Halicarnassus, one of the Seven Wonders of the Ancient World. Until 1964, it stood as the tallest structure in the city. It was therefore a prime target for destruction in *The War of the Worlds* (1953). The famous pyramid inspired top of the building gets done in by the Martians in a special-effects spectacular created pre-CGI with good old plaster. ✻

# GO FURTHER

*Recommended reading, useful websites and further viewing*

## BOOKS

**Designing Disney's Theme Parks:**
**The Architecture of Reassurance**
Edited by Karal Ann Marling
(Flammarion, 1997)

**The History of Forgetting:**
**Los Angeles and the Erasure of Memory**
By Norman M. Klein.
(Verso Books, 1997)

**Writing Los Angeles, A Literary Anthology**
Edited by David L. Olin
(Library of America, 2002)

**The Most Typical Avant-Garde:**
**History and Geograpohy of Minor Cinema**
**in Los Angeles**
By David E. James
(University of California Press, 2005)

**L.A. Noir: The City as Character**
By Alain Silver and James Ursini
(Santa Monica Press, 2006)

**Los Angeles: A City On Film**
Curated by Thom Andersen
(Vienna International Film Festival, 2008)

**Los Angeles, Portrait of a City**
By Jim Heimann, Kevin Starr
and David L. Ulin
(Taschen, 2009)

**Robert Altman: The Oral Biography**
By Mitchell Zuckoff
(Alfred A. Knopf, 2009)

**Hollywood Cinema and**
**the Real Los Angeles**
By Mark Shiel
(Reaktion Books, 2012)

## BOOKS (CONTINUED)

**Los Angeles Boulevard:**
**Eight X-Rays of the Body Public**
By Doug Suisman
(Oro editions, 2014)

**Jet Age Aesthetic:**
**The Glamour of Media in Motion**
By Vanessa R. Schwartz
(Yale University Press, 2020)

**Paul Thomas Anderson: Masterworks**
By Adam Nayman
(Little White Lies, 2020)

**A Cultural History of the Disneyland**
**Theme Parks: Middle Class Kingdoms**
By Sabrina Mittermeier
(Intellect Books, 2022)

## WEBSITES

**Wartime radio broadcast**
By Sir Winston Churchill
BBC (1 October 1939)
*http://tiny.cc/xmn6yz*

**'It's a dump they're going to miss'**
By Emily Otani
Los Angeles Times (29 November 1996)
*http://tiny.cc/rmn6yz*

**'"Meet me on main street":**
**Disneyland as place attachment for**
**Southern Californians'**
By William McCarthy
Tourism Geographies, 21:4 (2019), pp. 586–612
*http://tiny.cc/umn6yz*

**'The pedigree of pixie dust: Disneyland and**
**theme parks as a remediation of playful**
**places throughout history'**
By William McCarthy
Journal of Leisure Res., 53:2 (2022), pp. 253–71
*http://tiny.cc/wmn6yz*

# CONTRIBUTORS

*Editor and contributing writer biographies*

## EDITORS

**GABRIEL SOLOMONS** has over twenty years of experience in editorial production management, contract publishing and project facilitation for a range of clients including Sky Television, The V&A, MTV, California Tourism, AllCity Media, HotelMap and Brighton Museums & Galleries. As both a designer and university lecturer, he has delivered papers, workshops and speeches on design, film, publishing and book production at various venues worldwide. He is the editor and art-director of the fully illustrated movie magazine *Beneficial Shock!* and is also the founder and editor-in-chief of *The Big Picture* – an online film magazine and podcast.

**JARED COWAN** is a contributing writer and photographer for various Los Angeles-based publications. He has written extensively on the subject of LA filming locations for *Los Angeles Magazine*, *L.A. Weekly* and *L.A. TACO*. Jared podcasts about filming locations on his own show, *On Location with Jared Cowan*, in which he interviews filmmakers on-site at the locations from their movies. He also leads film tours of the San Fernando Valley, Pasadena and the historic Langham Huntington Hotel in Pasadena.

**FABRICE ZIOLKOWSKI** has been a writer-director for over forty years. Today, he mostly writes for animation and penned the Oscar-nominated *The Secret of Kells* (2010). He has also produced and directed documentaries on capital punishment, modern dance, The Beatles and Los Angeles. He has written for various publications on topics ranging from Marcel Proust to the Blues and is the author of the novel *Ashes 2 Ashes* (CreateSpace 2010).

## CONTRIBUTORS

**ROBERT FOULKES** was born, raised and lives in Los Angeles, a city he still loves. He has worked as a location manager for film and television for over thirty years, with credits that include *La La Land* (2016), *Three Billboards Outside Ebbing, Missouri* (2017) and *Ford v Ferrari* (2019). Robert is a member of the Location Managers Guild International (LMGI) and Production Design branch of the Academy of Motion Picture Arts

and Sciences. He also dabbles in screenwriting, which he hopes to focus on more if he can ever find the time! www.imdb.com/name/nm0288316/

**GEORGINA GUTHRIE** is a freelance writer and journalist currently based in Bristol. Her writing on film and culture has appeared in *Little White Lies*, *The Quietus* and *Time Out* among others. She has previously edited Intellect Ltd's *The Big Picture* magazine website, and curated several short film nights in her hometown of Bristol.

**DAVID E. JAMES** was born in the Nottinghamshire village of Laxton, the only place where the communal, three-field system of farming, once ubiquitous over western Europe, still exists. After a few ups and many downs, he became a professor at the University of Southern California. His teaching and research interests focused on avant-garde cinema, culture in Los Angeles, East-Asian cinema, cinema and music, and working-class culture. His books include *Written Withing and Without: A Reading of Blake's Milton*; *Allegories of Cinema: American Film in the Sixties*; *The Most Typical Avant-Garde: History and Geography of Minor Cinemas in Los Angeles*; and *Rock 'N' Film: Cinema's Dance with Popular Music*, together with six edited collections, including *Optic Antics: The Cinema of Ken Jacobs* and *Alternative Projections: Experimental Film in Los Angeles, 1945-1980*. On retiring in 2020, he published his last collection of essays, *Power Misses II: Cinema Asian and Modern*. Since then, he has been occupied with film and photo projects about Laxton specifically and, more generally, the struggle of commons against empire.

**DAVID B. LYONS** is a location manager and scout in the Los Angeles area. Raised in Southwest Michigan, David moved to Los Angeles in 2003 to pursue a job in film and has been working in locations since 2005. His location credits include numerous TV series and feature films and he has won several awards for his work. David is also part of the group that made the show *Yacht Rock* (2005–2010) which is responsible for the term used by countless DJ's and cover bands to this day. www.imdb.com/name/nm1502835/

# CONTRIBUTORS

*Editor and contributing writer biographies (continued)*

**NEIL MITCHELL** is the editor of the London and Melbourne editions of the *World Film Locations* series and co-editor of *Directory of World Cinema: Britain* (2012) all published by Intellect Books. His monograph on Brian De Palma's *Carrie* was published by Auteur as → part of its Devil's Advocates series. Neil has contributed to *Total Film*, *Electric Sheep*, *Eye For Film* and *New Empress*.

**ANDREW NOCK** has written, produced and directed a wide variety of TV shows and documentaries all over the world. From life and death struggles in the developing countries, to the search for the Zodiac Killer, and the truth behind the UFO Phenomena. Andrew was born in Durham, England. In the 1990s, he followed his passion for film by moving to Los Angeles and started Levitation Productions based in the San Fernando Valley.

**ADA PÎRVU** writes the online cultural publication *Classiq Journal*, channeling her passion for cinema, photography and storytelling. A regular contributor to various film and art magazines around the world, Ada is a firm believer in a well-cultured life, one in which day-dreaming, creativity and authenticity play centre role.

**THOMAS M. PUHR** lives in Chicago, Illinois, where he teaches English and Language Arts. He is the editor of online film magazine *The Big Picture* and has worked as a copy editor for the *Journal of Global Social Work Practice*. His work has also appeared in *Bright Lights Film Journal* and *The Open End*. In addition to writing short stories, plays and screenplays, he enjoys updating his film blog, Screen Icebergs and recently completed his first book *Fate in Film: A Deterministic Approach to Cinema* (2022), which was published by Columbia University Press.

**PETER SCHULMAN** is a professor of French and international studies at Old Dominion University where he has been named an 'Eminent Scholar'. He also has been designated an Officier des Palmes Academiques by the French Government. Professor Schulman serves on the Board of Trustees of the North American Jules Verne Society (NAJVS) and is a worldwide Jules Verne scholar. He is the editor of Verne's *The Begum's Millions* (Wesleyan University Press, 2014) and has translated his last novel, *The Secret of Wilhelm Storitz* (University of Nebraska Press, 2011) as well as *A Thousand and Second Night and Other Plays* (BearManor Media, 2018) by Jules Verne. In addition to his work on Verne, he has also co-authored *Le Dernier Livre du Siècle* (ROMILLAT, 2004) and translated eight books of French poetry and non-fiction.

**DAVID WASCO**, production designer, and **SANDY REYNOLDS-WASCO**, set decorator, are a husband and wife duo who have worked together on more than 39 feature films in the past 40 years. They have collaborated with some of the most talented filmmakers today, including Quentin Tarantino, Wes Anderson, Michael Mann, Paul Schrader, David Mamet and most recently Damien Chazelle and Aaron Sorkin. David and Sandy won the 2016 Academy Award for Best Achievement in Production Design, the Art Directors Guild Award for Excellence in Production Design and a BAFTA nomination for Best Production Design for their work on Damien Chazelle's *La La Land* (2016). After working with Quentin Tarantino on *Reservoir Dogs* in 1992, they continued working with him, designing *Pulp Fiction* (1994), *Jackie Brown* (1998), *Kill Bill: Vol. 1* (2003) and *Vol. 2* (2004) and *Inglourious Basterds* (2009), which received the BAFTA nomination for Best Production Design. Wasco's design work on Wes Anderson's *The Royal Tenenbaums* (2001) was featured in the Smithsonian's National Design Triennial in 2003.

**ALBERTO ZAMBENEDETTI** is an associate professor in the Department of Italian Studies and the Cinema Studies Institute at the University of Toronto. He is the author of *Acting Across Borders: Mobility and Identity in Italian Cinema* (Edinburgh University Press, 2021), and the editor of *World Film Locations: Florence* (Intellect Books, 2014) and *World Film Locations: Cleveland* (Intellect Books, 2016). Alberto is a cat person.

# FILMOGRAPHY

*A comprehensive list of all films mentioned or featured in this volume*

| | |
|---|---|
| A Better Life (2011) | 89, 96 |
| A Woman Under the Influence (1974) | 14 |
| Assault on Precinct 13 (1976) | 9, 18 |
| Back to the Future (1985) | 108 |
| Ballet Mécanique (1924) | 26 |
| Barbie (2023) | III, 128 |
| Barfly (1987) | 49, 56 |
| Barton Fink (1991) | 7 |
| Battle: Los Angeles (2011) | 131 |
| Beginners (2010) | 89, 92 |
| Birth of A Nation (1915) | 10, 109 |
| Boogie Nights (1997) | 108, 109 |
| Booksmart (2019) | III, 122 |
| Bowfinger (1999) | 69, 80 |
| Bush Mama (1976) | 27 |
| Clambake (1967) | 108 |
| Corvette Summer (1978) | 109 |
| Dazed and Confused (1993) | 87 |
| Destroyer (2018) | III, 116 |
| Dope (2015) | 89, 104 |
| Drive (2011) | 108 |
| Duel in the Sun (1946) | 109 |
| E.T. the Extra-Terrestrial (1982) | 108 |
| Earthquake (1974) | 131 |
| El Valley Centro (1999) | 27 |
| Falling Down (1993) | 86 |
| Fast Times at Ridgemont High (1982) | 29, 38, 42, 108 |
| Fragment of Seeking (1946) | 26 |
| Grand Canyon 1991 | 69, 74 |
| Greenberg (2010) | 86, 89, 90 |
| Heaven Can Wait (1978) | 9, 22 |
| Hito Hata: Raise the Banner (1980) | 27 |
| Independence Day (1996) | 131 |
| Intolerance (1916) | 9, 10 |
| Killer of Sheep (1977) | 27 |
| Kiss Me Deadly (1955) | 131 |
| L.A. Plays Itself (1972) | 27 |
| L.A.X. (1980) | 27, 29, 30 |
| La La Land (2016) | 7, III, 112, 133, 134 |
| Less Than Zero (1987) | 49, 58 |
| Licorice Pizza (2021) | 109, III, 126 |
| Los (2000) | 27 |
| Los Angeles Plays Itself (2003) | 27 |
| M*A*S*H (1970) | 6, 7 |
| Magnolia (1999) | 109 |
| Manzanar (1971) | 27 |
| Meshes of the Afternoon (1943) | 26 |
| Miracle Mile (1988) | 49, 64, 130 |
| Mulholland Drive (2001) | 87 |
| Mur Murs (1981) | 29, 32 |
| Night of the Comet (1984) | 49, 50, 131 |
| Night Tide (1960) | 26 |
| Nightcrawler (2014) | 89, 102 |
| On the Edge (1949) | 26 |
| Once Upon A Time in Hollywood (2019) | 109, III, 120 |
| Panic in Year Zero (1962) | 131 |
| Picnic (1948) | 26 |
| Promising Young Woman (2020) | III, 124 |
| Punch-Drunk Love (2002) | 84, 109, 126 |
| Repo Man (1984) | 29, 44 |
| Requiem 29 (1971) | 27 |
| Short Cuts (1993) | 6, 7 |
| Sleeping Beauty (1959) | 46 |
| Sodom and Gomorrah (1962) | 130 |
| Sogobi (2002) | 27 |
| Song of the South (1946) | 46 |
| Stagecoach (1939) | 109 |
| Sunset Boulevard (1950) | 7, 66 |
| Tangerine (2015) | 89, 106 |
| The Big Knife (1955) | 7 |
| The Day of the Locust (1975) | 9, 16 |
| The Decline of Western Civilization (1981) | 29, 34 |
| The Flying Deuces (1939) | 109 |
| The Karate Kid (1984) | 49, 52, 108 |
| The Life and Death of 9413: A Hollywood Extra (1928) | 26 |
| The Long Goodbye (1973) | 6, 108 |
| The Maltese Falcon (1941) | 67 |
| The Neon Demon (2016) | III, 114 |
| The Other Side of Madness (1971) | 109 |
| The Player (1992) | 6, 7 |
| The Princess and the Frog (2009) | 46 |
| The Savage Eye (1960) | 9, 14, 26 |
| The Soul of the Cypress (1920) | 26 |
| The State of Things (1982) | 29, 36 |
| The War of the Worlds (1953) | 64, 131 |
| They Live! (1988) | 49, 62 |
| This Is the End (2013) | 131 |
| Touch of Evil (1958) | 7, 9, 12 |
| Training Day (2001) | 69, 82, 98 |
| Twilight (1998) | 66, 67 |
| Under the Silver Lake (2018) | 87, III, 118 |
| Valley Girl (1983) | 29, 42, 108 |
| Van Nuys Blvd. (1979) | 109 |
| Water and Power (1998) | 27 |
| Water Ritual # 1: An Urban Rite of Purification (1980) | 27 |